D0069293

LOST IN TOKYO

A Year of Sex, Sushi, and Suicide in the Real Japan

Garett Wilson

Shinden Press

Tokyo

Copyright © 2018 Garett Wilson.

All rights reserved. No part of this publication may be reproduced, distributed, or transmitted in any form or by any means, including photocopying, recording, or other electronic or mechanical methods, without the prior written permission of the authors, except in the case of brief quotations embodied in critical reviews and certain other non-commercial uses permitted by copyright law.

Second printing, 2018.

Shinden Press

Tokyo

Japan

Contents

He Brought a Snake to School 5

Sweat and Panic 13

Mr Foreigner 18

Nice to Meet You 24

What Do You Think of My Playboy Socks? 28

These Are My Children 35

It's a Strange Place 39

Do You Eat Fish Abroad? 43

Zoe Wannamaker and John Hurt 50

That Class Is Pretty Stupid 55

Heil Hitler 61

He Said I Was Going Bald 65

A Lasso in the Eye 69

You're a Waste of Space 75

Where the Hell Are You? 80

Oh Shit, I'm Fallin' in Love 84

Very Countryside 90

Laundry Detergent for Half-Wits 95

Just Like Vegas 98

Superman and Keystone Cops 102

Tokyo Land 106

Undead Horse Mackerel 112

She Loves You 118

You Need Them More Than Me 126

Television Was Watched by Me 129

Skimpy Sumo-Style Underpants   135

Terminal   140

A Detective Who is Actually a Dog in Human Form   147

Look at His Tall Nose   153

No Pets, No Foreigners   160

Why Would She Be Here?   168

It's Complicated   176

Stay or Rest?   182

I've Had Enough of This   188

Career Suicide   196

A Beautiful Heart   203

It Looks Really Bad   211

It Might Hurt a Bit   217

Enjoy a KFC Christmas   224

You're Very Athletic   229

Work-Life Balance   237

Yamada Kun   242

Salt-Flavoured Suit   251

A Scene from Blade Runner   257

Is This My Salary?   263

Stand Up, Bow and Sit Down   269

About the Author   274

He Brought a Snake to School

On the greyest of mornings, a lone figure trudged slowly over the bridge. He was hunched under his rusty umbrella, glancing at a soggy photocopied map and barely noticing the last of the cherry blossoms as the rain eased them off their branches. Through the drizzle, the massive orange skeleton of Tokyo Tower was just visible behind rows of skyscrapers. If this were a film, the director would be lauded for creating a shot that conveyed so much in one frame. Unfortunately, this was real life and that lone figure was me.

I straightened my tie for the twelfth time since leaving the station and wondered if I should have gone for a more conservative colour. I cursed myself for not polishing my shoes but was glad that the rain had given them a passable sheen. Just to be sure, I dipped the toes in a puddle, and discovered that they were no longer waterproof. I reached the end of the bridge, and a last look at the map told me that the modern brown brick tower to the right was the place. The Big Ben-imitation chimes rang. I was just on time as I saw Ms Shinohara, the dispatch agency's representative, at the front gate. I had met her once before, at the three-day orientation and training seminar supposed to prepare me for all the eventualities of life as an Assistant Language Teacher (ALT) at a Japanese junior high school. She looked relieved to see me now, as if she hadn't really believed I would show up.

'You're here,' she said cheerfully, then saved me from thinking up a suitable response to such a statement of the obvious, by adding, 'Are you ready?' She led me inside to the eerily quiet reception area. 'The students don't start until tomorrow,' she told me. 'Today is just a chance for you to meet the Principal and the other teachers. Have you got your indoor shoes?'

'Sorry?'

'Indoor shoes. You can't wear those in the building.'

After four years in Japan I was used to the very sensible custom of taking off shoes when entering houses and even some restaurants, but it had never occurred to me that the same rules would apply to a place of work. My previous jobs had been in 'conversation schools' where office workers and housewives spent millions of yen to study English and gain a taste of foreign culture, and shoes were kept firmly on.

'There are some slippers over there.'

As I took off my shoes I realised just how wet my socks were and silently prayed that the damp stench wasn't too obvious. I squeezed on the tiny red slippers, my heels hanging uncomfortably over the rear edge of the soles. I clenched my toes to try and grip onto the leather but with every step the slippers would slide off, forcing me to shuffle along the freshly-waxed floor like a geisha girl. Ms Shinohara wore similar slippers but moved effortlessly as she ushered me to hurry up. I made a mental note to buy some indoor shoes that evening.

We took some stairs to the second floor, a process lengthened by the occasional need to retrieve stray footwear, then met two members of the local ward's Board of Education outside the Principal's office. I recognised them from my interview – a dreadful experience compounded by the fact that I had been told by my agency that the job was at a *senior* high school (for students aged fifteen to eighteen). The truth only became apparent after I'd delivered a carefully-prepared speech about the importance of priming students for university entrance exams.

'You do know that the students are twelve to fifteen years old, don't you? It's at least three years before those tests.'

'Umm… It's never too early to start.'

And when they had asked me if I could speak Japanese, I'd said yes, meaning that I was more than capable of communicating with colleagues and friends. Unfortunately, they took it as meaning I was happy to perform the rest of the interview in the language. I quickly found out that teaching philosophies and the vagaries of English grammar aren't the easiest topics of discussion in a foreign tongue.

Still, I can't have done that badly as here we were. For the first time in ten years, I was going through the familiar teenage hell of waiting outside the Principal's office.

The usual Japanese small talk settled my nerves a little before the two Education Board members began umm-ing and ahh-ing. Ms Shinohara asked if everything was OK, and they looked at each other, then at me, before whispering apologetically.

'The Principal is new. He has his own ideas, and…'

The office door opened and a gruff man in late middle age muttered permission for us to enter.

The first thing that struck me was the size of the office. For a moment I wondered if it was the staffroom, lined as it was with armchairs for a dozen or more people and headed by a large desk. A trophy cabinet sparkled with cups and shields and the walls were decorated with beautifully framed reproductions of Gauguins, Renoirs and Picassos. Photos of school trips to Australia were dotted around the room. Situated in one of the more affluent wards of central Tokyo, a combination of big business and sparse population made for a lot of tax money to be spent on a few students. This office wouldn't have been out of place on the top floor of a multi-national corporation's HQ. I think I would have found that less intimidating.

The Principal, a muscular former PE teacher, asked us to sit down and we sank into the ludicrously low armchairs. If I didn't know better I would have sworn they'd been designed that way, to make people like me feel small and insignificant. All I needed was a flat cap to shift nervously through my fingers.

The Principal sat on the wooden arm of a chair opposite me, blocking out a lamp behind him and casting a wide shadow that swallowed me up. We went through further pleasantries, everyone but me having a business card to present to one another. These cards are shrouded in strict protocol: with both parties bowing, the card must always be passed face-up and the right way round to be read by the recipient. This person then makes a point of examining (or at least pretending to examine) the information – nothing more exciting than name, title and contact details. They then place it carefully into a small wallet before reciprocating. With the Principal, Vice-Principal, two Board of Education representatives and Ms Shinohara in the room, this process took some time and I was feeling increasingly left out when all I could offer was my name. I made a mental note of something else to buy that evening.

Just as I was beginning to doze off, the formalities ended and we were joined by two women, both in their early forties, who I was introduced to as the JTEs (Japanese Teachers of English). Ms Hasebe was marginally attractive, spoke near-perfect English with a slight North American accent, and smiled and nodded in all the right places. Ms Ikuta, on the other hand, looked at me suspiciously with a sour expression. She didn't use any English; in fact, she didn't address me directly at all, and every question went to poor Ms Shinohara.

As the conversation went on, my heart went out to the agency rep' more and more. I had presumed she was an old hand at these meetings but it soon became apparent that she was just a part-timer, a retiree who earned a bit of pocket money this time of year by escorting people like me to their new placements. She fielded the questions to the best of her ability but ultimately could only say, 'Please call the agency.' And all this time I'd been thinking she *was* the agency. Still, my sympathies can only extend so far, and I was a lot more concerned about my own plight.

At first the Principal gave all the usual platitudes about the importance of arriving on time, working hard and occasionally giving a bit extra. Again, none of these were aimed directly at me, and I felt a bit like a child being discussed by his parents, my head turning left and right, trying to keep up as the conversation rattled along. Little by little, the Principal became more agitated as he began talking about his expectations of an ALT. Ms Shinohara was rapidly translating, a relief as the Principal's speech was coarse and fast and I was only able to catch fragments. 'At my last school, the ALT just messed around... He sat on the desk in class, like this.' He mimed a hands-in-pockets slouch. 'He was always shouting and screaming... He brought a snake to school.' I hoped this was just a toy. 'He waved it in the kids' faces to get their attention.' By now he was in full flow, his finger pointing an inch from my nose. I think I'd preferred it when he was grilling Ms Shinohara. I must have looked like a rabbit in headlights, and those around me weren't faring much better. 'You're here to work! You're here to teach! No silly games! You're not a clown! Do you understand?' I managed a whimper as I wiped his spittle from my left eye. 'DO YOU UNDERSTAND?!' I nodded, convinced that if I tried to speak I'd end up crying.

Thank God for Mr Arakawa, the Vice Principal. He took over at this point, and he is one of those people who just exudes warmth. I think he felt a little embarrassed for his new boss's outburst and decided to ease the tension by telling me about the family atmosphere around the school and how much fun the sports day and culture festival would be. The way I was feeling I just wanted to hug him, but I wasn't sure that would go down too well with everyone so

I just carried on nodding until I could feel my strength returning.

Finally, Mr Arakawa beckoned me through a side door to the staffroom, along with the rest of my ever-increasing entourage, although I noticed that the Principal stayed in his office, as if he didn't want to be connected with me in any way. The staffroom was much as I had expected. My parents were both secondary school teachers so I was used to the sight of desks heaving under the untidy weight of books, test papers and laptops. The requisite stained coffee cups were present and correct, and I was glad to see a small kitchen area in the corner, well-stocked with snacks.

The Vice-Principal called for everyone's attention. Silence fell and twenty sets of eyes turned towards me. If the Principal had turned me white with terror, the blood was fast returning to my cheeks. 'This is Ga… Ga…'

'Garett,' I helped out. While not very common, mine is a fairly straightforward name in English but the cause of all kinds of difficulties in Japan where consonant clusters are rare. The closest approximation in the phonetic *katakana* alphabet seems to be *Garetto*, though my football friends insisted on *Garetsu*. People often asked me which it should be, as if my parents were considering the Japanese pronunciation when they were thinking up baby names in the early eighties, on the off-chance I'd end up living in Tokyo.

'Garett sensei,' Mr Arakawa confirmed, adding the honorific that always pleases me – it makes me feel like a wizened old karate master.

'Nice to meet you all. I'm from Britain. I've been teaching

English in Japan for four years but this is my first time in a junior high school. I look forward to working with you.'

I had phrased it in the most polite Japanese I knew but it had all come out in one nervous blurt. Thankfully, the bows and murmurs of understanding told me that I'd got my message across, and everyone got back to work. Ms Ikuta went back to her desk without so much as a word of encouragement and Ms Hasebe went to hers with a quick, 'See you tomorrow.' The Vice-Principal led me back into the Principal's office. He gave a cursory nod and then I was out of the door along with Ms Shinohara and the Education Board staff. Much to my surprise, my first day had lasted exactly twenty minutes.

My mind was still spinning as we walked back over the bridge towards the Metro station. Ms Shinohara promised to tell the agency how aggressive the Principal appeared to be, and the Board of Education members kept repeating the mantra, 'He's new, he's new.' Friends later told me that he had probably just had bad experiences with foreign ALTs previously so felt the need to lay down the law; I shouldn't take it personally. But if he had met, say, a bad history teacher in his old school, would that cause him to yell at every history teacher he met from then on? As I took the train home and the sweat on my back slowly dried, all I could do was dread the next day and the months ahead.

Sweat and Panic

If first impressions count, then new jobs are designed to win us as few friends as possible. I'm prone to insomnia at the best of times but the night before a major event I can pretty much give up on getting any sleep altogether. I'm a creature of habit and a new morning routine is always difficult to become accustomed to. My previous job usually started around eleven a.m., so I could doze blissfully through my girlfriend's morning rituals before pottering around the flat as I pleased. But now our schedules were almost identical – the seven o'clock alarm followed by a battle for the shower, for the toilet, for the bathroom sink, even for the TV remote. This would take some getting used to. A hurried shave left my neck dotted with blood and I was still wiping toothpaste off my chin as I ran for the train.

This journey would become second nature soon enough but here it came as a terrible shock. The walk-cum-run to Hirai station was easy enough as we had made a point of renting an apartment just two minutes away. The street was more crowded than I had ever seen it before and it occurred to me that this was my first taste of the rush hour in Tokyo. Until now I had always worked the irregular hours that conversation schools demand – midday starts, late-night finishes and weekend work. It was nice to finally have a similar schedule to my friends and girlfriend; the downside was having a similar schedule to everyone else in the biggest metropolis in the world. Just walking along the platform was difficult, it was so full of commuters. 'Accident' is the euphemism usually reserved for someone jumping onto the tracks in one of the most selfish and far-reaching forms of suicide – scores of people are mentally scarred by the very public and unpleasant death; thousands of commuters are stranded while the track is cleared of human debris, leaving hundreds of businesses and services short-staffed; and the family of the victim is sued by the rail company for its losses. But I'm amazed that there aren't more *real* accidents as the crowd teeters on the edge of the platform and trains whiz in and out of the station every minute.

I squeezed myself into the carriage, my legs almost being lifted off the floor by the mass of people, and tried to make myself comfortable. This was no easy task with an elbow jammed in my back and someone's dandruff-covered shoulder tucked under my nose. It was another chilly morning but the train felt like a rainforest, the air thick and damp with sweat. As we stopped at each station there was a rugby-style rolling maul off the carriage, sometimes carrying me with it, forcing me to battle my way back on. It really is testament to the placid nature of most Japanese people that there aren't more fights each morning – it pains me to say that a similar situation back home would almost certainly end in scrapping and brawling. But here the commuters seemed able to block out all the discomfort, serene expressions contrasting with the anger welling up inside me.

At Ryogoku station I was able to alight and, after

maneuvering my way out of the building, the first blast of fresh air was wonderful. I'd only been out of the house ten minutes but I really needed a coffee. Luckily, a vending machine is always close by and I could grab a can of European Blend, a sickly sweet concoction vaguely resembling café au lait, to drink as I walked to the underground Metro. I didn't know then that, like an addict with a cigarette, I would never again be able to make that walk without a canned coffee in my hand.

The ten-minute stroll came as a relief after the stuffiness of the train, a chance to cool down and gather my thoughts. My gloom at facing the Principal was lightened by the sight of a sumo wrestler in a traditional *yukata* robe riding a tiny *mama-chari* – 'Mama chariot', a bicycle with a basket at the front – while chatting on his mobile phone, and I remembered that the sport's national stadium was just around the corner. He was on his way to the office, just like me.

The Metro was less crowded and I was even able to read a book on the train, something that had been impossible on the overland line earlier. However, the dark of the underground tunnel brought back the pang of foreboding. I was unable to concentrate on the plot of the novel so I resorted to counting down the stops. My station arrived far too soon. I realised I was running late so I jumped off the train and broke into a jog. After making the same trip the day before I felt confident of finding the way without a map. Unfortunately, this confidence was entirely unfounded, and you would think that a lifetime of getting lost would have opened my eyes to the fact that I have no sense of direction whatsoever. With the crowds of commuters milling around, everything seemed to look different from before and, after a few false starts, I checked an information board. Exit A1, it said, so I followed the arrows that way. I turned left – a long corridor; I turned right – another long corridor; I turned right again – the longest corridor ever built by man. I sprinted down it, then turned left, then rode the escalator; right – more steps; another right – even more steps, but also rays of sunlight. Free at last! I now had just five minutes to cross that bridge and get to school.

I trotted along the street. I'd be able to see the bridge any moment…

Where the hell was that damn bridge?

I was walking on the wrong road. I listened for the flow of water, eventually finding the river, and from there I could see the bridge. By now I was running full pelt, my bag sliding off my shoulder. I saw a few teenagers wearing what I guessed was the uniform of my new school. These students' first sight of Garett sensei was a blur of ruddy cheeks, sweat and panic.

At the entrance hall I met the caretaker, Ogata, similar age to me with a shy smile. He showed me my shoe locker and I changed out of my outdoor shoes and into my shiny new indoor ones. I bounded up the stairs, took a couple of deep breaths then knocked on the Principal's door. He grunted what may have been 'Good morning', pointed to a chair then went back to reading the newspaper. A clock ticked loudly. I tried to calm down and took my jacket off. I draped it over the arm of the chair but it slid to the floor. The Principal looked at me over the rim of his spectacles. I smiled. He went back to his paper and the clock ticked on.

Also waiting in his office were three children. They looked older than first years but their stiff, clean uniforms suggested they were new to the school. I said hello. They bowed politely. My general policy is to use only English with my students, but I made an exception in this case – they looked terrified enough already.

'Is it your first day?'

'Yes.'

I leaned in conspiratorially. 'Mine too.' An exchange straight out of one of my favourite films, *Goodbye Mr Chips!* I don't know how it made the students feel, but it relaxed me a little. My good humour did not last long.

Mr Foreigner

'*Gaijin san.*' It was the Principal, using a term that translates as 'Mr Foreigner' and is just as rude in either language. 'Go with Ms Hasebe.' The JTE was standing in the doorway. She took me through to the staffroom, showed me to my seat and I was thrilled to have – for the first time in my life – my very own desk, even if it was mostly covered in Ms Hasebe's stuff. She sat adjacent and it was clear that she would be my immediate supervisor. A cup of hot green tea was waiting for me, a daily offering from the school support staff. I said hello to the other teachers at the long bank of desks and at least two of them reciprocated.

Between consultations with other colleagues, Ms Hasebe filled me in on the day's schedule, beginning with the traditional start-of-term ceremony where the second and third year students welcome the first years into the school. The parents would be there too, so everyone would be on their best behaviour. This would be followed by cleaning.

'By the students?'

'Of course.' In Japan, the children are expected to maintain the upkeep of the building through daily cleaning of all classrooms, corridors and toilets.

'I'm going to be busy so just make sure you're in the sports hall at nine o'clock for the ceremony. The teachers' seats are at the front.' She dashed to another meeting and I was left, once again, sitting on my own and not knowing what to do. I played with my new desk, particularly enjoying the rolling drawers and secret compartments. They were packed full of old flashcards presumably made by the previous ALT but filed randomly with no discernible method of organisation: body parts were mixed in with photocopied US dollars, sports jumbled with food and drink. At least making sense of it all killed half an hour until it was time for me to join the ceremony.

I asked Ms Ishii, the mouse-like science teacher, where the sports hall was. She blushed, laughed and pointed me to another teacher. Despite my asking the question in Japanese, she couldn't believe that I would possibly understand her reply. This was to become a frustratingly common occurrence. Her fellow scientist, Mr Nakamura, was a jovial man with a smattering of English, and he kindly led me to the lift and told me to go to the sixth floor. As I got to see a little more of the school, I noticed that the art reproductions were everywhere, each on thick canvas in a heavy wooden frame. It was like working in the Louvre. The elevator, too, gave me a hint to the money behind the school, and was a welcome sight in a seven-storey building.

I came out on the sixth floor and the sports hall was straight ahead. The dusty, leathery smell was exactly the same as the gym in my old school in England. I never knew stenches could be so international. Inside were rows of students and parents but – I realised too late – no teachers. By the time I noticed, I was already well into the room, walking up the centre aisle in full and very conspicuous view of everyone. It was a minute to nine so I hoped that the other staff would come along shortly, and I sat down in the block of teachers' chairs. I tried to look professional but relaxed, a tricky business with three hundred people staring at me and whispering behind their hands. Every one of my movements felt clumsy and obvious. I became horribly aware of a nose hair dangling, tickling my nostril. I wanted to rip it out but had to sit on my hands and try not to think about it. The shaving rash on my neck was burning, my buttocks couldn't find a comfortable spot on the chair, and was that the first tingling of a need to pee? I remembered all the coffee and tea I'd drunk. But, according to Ms Hasebe, the ceremony would be starting any moment so I wouldn't have time to run out to the toilet. I judged it would be safer to stay put.

This dragged on for forty-five minutes.

Finally, the other teachers walked in and took their seats near me. Ms Hasebe sat by my side. 'You found the place, then.'

'Actually, I've been here since nine.'

She laughed condescendingly. 'That was the time for the students to be here, not us.'

'But you told me to come here at nine o'clock.'

She gave another patronising smile and shook her head slightly, as if to say, 'You're an idiot but I'll tolerate you as it's your first day.' I wanted to scream. It was a feeling that would become all too familiar.

The ceremony began with some speeches to the second and

third years before the new pupils marched in to Elgar's *Pomp and Circumstance*. I felt a twinge of nostalgia as I saw their crisp, oversized uniforms and wetted-down cowlicks of hair, their parents obviously keen to make them look as respectable as possible. I remembered my own parents' efforts to clean and preen me when I entered secondary school, despite all my best efforts to appear rough and ready.

The girls' uniform was the ubiquitous *sera-fuku* – sailor costume – derived from 1920s Royal Navy ceremonial clothing, while the boys wore *gakuran* high-collared jackets, based on those worn by the Prussian armed forces during Japan's period of modernisation at the end of the nineteenth century when a pot pourri of Western customs was adopted indiscriminately. For a country with no official army, militaristic fashions are very common.

Some students looked frightened, some delighted at entering The Big School. It was spookily easy to tell which ones would be the good kids, which ones bad, which ones the leaders and which ones the potential victims, and once again I was surprised by the similarities between Japanese and British students. Behind the superficial physical differences lay the same desires and concerns, the same sense of mischief one would expect from a twelve-year-old, wherever they came from.

Further speeches (the Principal was in terrifyingly aggressive form, his attempts at encouragement sounding like the threats of a dictator) were followed by the official presentation of the new teachers – another unpleasant shock. Ms Hasebe told me to follow the other fresh blood onto the stage, and I was left in a dilemma: If I used Japanese to introduce myself would I be discouraging students from speaking to me in English, before I'd even met them properly? But if I used my own language would I come across as arrogant and culturally insensitive in front of the parents and staff? And would the students understand me? On top of that, I was concentrating hard on standing properly – not too casual, not too stiff. My hands felt huge and ungainly so I linked them in front of my waist to try and prevent them from swaying. Suddenly the Vice-Principal called my name, I gave an instinctive English hello, and I'm ashamed to say that I then resorted to a horribly banal phrase, usually uttered by grinning buffoons on language-learning TV programmes: 'Let's speak English together.' I've no idea where it came from, and even as I said it I cringed, but it was too late. I then bowed, my hands still linked at the front. Afterwards, Ms Hasebe took great glee in telling me that this was a distinctly female way of bowing so, as well as sounding like an idiot, I had also given the Japanese equivalent of a dainty curtsy in front of the entire school population, and their families.

A seemingly simple act, bowing is actually quite a subtle art and one that I continue to struggle with. I can never get the line of my back and neck straight enough, and my arms always dangle awkwardly (I've since learned that a man should keep his hands to the side). Different angles of bow signify different levels of feeling, from a slight tilt of the head as a morning greeting to a ninety-degree bend of abject apology. If you're in real trouble, then you can opt for a kneeling bow, hands and forehead touching the floor in front, but thankfully this is now usually reserved for television comedies. One of my previous conversation schools was situated in a shopping centre, and in the staff canteen was a full-length mirror etched with lines showing the angle of bow required for welcoming, thanking and saying sorry to customers. I always chuckled at shop staff practising in front of it, but now I wish I'd paid a bit more attention.

The ceremony continued and I'd never had to stand up and sit down so frequently. This, of course, was all very natural for the teachers and students and they followed the cues easily, but I must have looked like Corporal Jones from *Dad's Army* as my movements lagged half a second behind everyone else's. At one point I saw the students standing up so I quickly followed, only to find all the teachers next to me still seated. It wasn't the start I was hoping for.

Nice to Meet You

I was relieved when the ceremony came to a close, not least because I really was desperate for the toilet by then, two hours after that first tingle of possibility. I found the staff bathroom and had yet another flashback to my own student days – the feeling of refuge an empty boys' room can bring. After a gloriously relaxing pee, I splashed some water on my face and finally plucked that irritating nose hair. It was time now to face the students for real in *osouji* – cleaning time.

Ms Hasebe, whose word I was beginning to seriously doubt, told me to help the third years take their chairs and desks to their new classrooms. When I arrived at their old room they were already almost finished. The desks were very light so most students could manage to take them in one trip and there was nothing left for me to carry. Still, I took it as a good opportunity to get to know some of the kids so smiled and said hello to everyone I met. Most of them looked utterly bewildered that I would speak to them in English and I was beginning to wonder if 'Hello, nice to meet you' was too advanced for them. I shortened it to just 'Hello' but the puzzled expressions didn't change. The only variation on the theme was puzzlement coupled with contempt. I knew a junior high school was going to be a lot different from the conversation school atmosphere where motivated students were delighted to see me each week, but it still came as a genuine shock to be looked at with such unhidden disdain. I was glad when cleaning time was over and I could return to the staffroom.

The students went home at lunchtime and I felt that whoever made this schedule was putting off actually having to do any proper work. The first week was taken up almost entirely with ceremonies, meetings, picking up new materials (each student gets their own brand new copy of every textbook, a contrast to the decades-old, dog-eared books I had to use in school), choosing clubs and just about anything except the act of studying. It allowed me some time to get used to the building, familiarise myself with students' faces and get to know the other English teachers better, but also prevented me from establishing any routine.

Ms Hasebe continued to confound me with incorrect and unclear instructions and didn't stop talking about how wonderful my predecessor had been. Her catchphrase was 'Pete used to...' She constantly asked me questions but never listened to my answers, deciding instead to stereotype me as a lazy chancer who was in Japan on a working holiday, had no clue about 'real teaching', and could not understand any Japanese. This despite my telling her that I'd been in Japan for four years on a teacher's visa, was halfway through a Master's degree in English teaching and regularly studied Japanese.

Ms Ikuta, the other JTE, thawed out a little, at least passing the time of day, and I put her initial distant demeanour down to shyness. Her accent was clearly Japanese but her English, too, was excellent. This may seem a given for a junior high school English teacher, but I have met a lot of people in her position who have a solid grammar knowledge but struggle to communicate in a real conversation, a symptom of an education system based around rote learning and written tests and something that the introduction of foreign ALTs was designed to remedy.

The other staff buzzed around the staffroom and it was almost impossible to have any kind of genuine conversation. My attempts at small talk in the kitchen area were usually met with similar responses to Ms Ishii's – a flustered laugh and a bolt for freedom. Caucasians are still a relatively rare sight in Japan and I was well used to the occasional look of horror when I met people for the first time. Far from being resentful, it usually stemmed from embarrassment. Most people tend to presume that any white person must speak English (an understandable bug-bear for my French friend) and not know any Japanese so, even if I approach them in their own language, they often feel ashamed at what they perceive as their own weakness, poor English. I kept telling myself that it was not intended to sleight me. However, it did begin to grate when it happened a dozen times in a couple of days, particularly as all of the teachers would have worked with ALTs before. I often read about the East Asian need 'not to lose face' (usually in books written by Westerners), but what about the other person in these exchanges? By running away or blanking me, that person may save himself some embarrassment, but I'm left feeling like a prize idiot.

By the end of the week I gave up trying anything more daring than 'Nice day today' with the majority of my new colleagues.

What Do You Think of My Playboy Socks?

The following Monday, classes began in earnest. I was actually pleased to finally get into the classroom after all the procrastinating of the opening week. It had been very difficult to build any relationship with the students in the snatches of chat between presentations and preparations, so I was looking forward to discovering their English ability and getting to grips with a new way of working – Team Teaching. As I don't have a Japanese teaching certificate, I'm not legally allowed to teach in a state school without a JTE present. Theoretically, a foreign ALT is there to provide students with a window to the outside world, someone to practise English with, bolster their communicative skills and give some cultural background to the language. The Ministry of Education blurb talks of JTEs and ALTs working together to plan and carry out lessons in a way that increases students' confidence and conversation skills. The reality is often very different.

The majority of ALTs are recent graduates who plan to stay in Japan for just a year or two. They don't have any teaching experience or qualifications and cannot speak Japanese, and they often have no particular interest in education. I can understand the feeling of some JTEs who work very hard to gain full-time positions in schools (the tests required to gain a teaching certificate are notoriously difficult), only to have to share their role with a random person whose sole attribute is that they happen to come from another country. The unfortunate side-effect is that even those ALTs with a real interest in teaching are all too easily tarred with the same brush – as the Principal and Ms Hasebe's attitudes illustrated.

On the other hand, many JTEs have had no formal training in the art of team teaching. Some lack the English ability to communicate with the ALT comfortably and some simply lack the empathy to know how it feels to be a very clearly marked 'outsider' in a new environment. Without the means or confidence to talk openly, misunderstandings can easily occur. To avoid any difficult situations, some JTEs see the safer option as using the ALT sparingly, like a human tape recorder to read passages from the textbook, when a CD player would be a lot cheaper; or as an admin worker and manual helper, photocopying and carrying things but playing little part in the lessons themselves. Others may take an opposite approach, expecting the ALT to have an array of activities ready at a moment's notice then showing great dismay when the ALT is flummoxed by the request.

As with most things in life, it all comes down to the individuals involved, and I was to experience the best and worst of team teaching in the next few months.

Japanese students spend most of their school day at one desk, these lined in neat rows, all facing the huge blackboard. Apart from specialist subjects such as science and PE, it is the teachers who have to walk from classroom to classroom during the ten-minute intervals between each lesson, as opposed to Western students traipsing to different teachers' rooms for each class. The Japanese way makes more sense to me. Better to have a handful of teachers roaming the corridors every hour than three hundred kids; and there is no excuse for forgetting books and stationery because it should all be in the student's desk. The downside, especially when I hadn't set foot in a secondary school since my A-levels, was the psychological upper hand the students had over the teachers entering their patch. It's quite daunting the first time you see thirty sullen teenagers staring at you when you walk into their room.

The traditional way to begin a lesson is by the students standing up on the command of the class leader. These leaders play an important role in the school, expected to liaise with teachers and set an example for their peers. In this school the prerequisite for such an exalted position appeared to be baseball club membership. The students should then bow and bark *'Onegaishimasu'*, literally meaning 'please' but in this case extending to, 'Please teach us.' The teacher bows in return, the students sit down and the lesson can begin. Ms Ikuta preferred an English opening, the students still standing but saying 'Good morning' and answering a couple of simple questions before being asked to sit. Ms Hasebe told the students, 'English greetings are childish,' but didn't seem to like the Japanese kind either so the lessons started with a confusing mix of bows from the geeky kids, some general chatter from the others and no-one really certain whether the class had begun or not.

As an opening gambit with the second and third years I prepared an activity whereby I write a few sentences about myself on the blackboard, for example, 'I like football and rugby' and 'I'm from the UK.' The students should then think of questions to match the answers. In these cases, 'What sport do you like?' and 'Where are you from?' A pretty simple task, and one that I had used successfully with seven-year-olds in my previous job. Luckily for those seven-year-olds, Ms Hasebe wasn't in the room with them. She insisted on translating every word I said, then adding another five minutes of her own views on the subject. I said 'I don't like *natto* (fermented beans that smell like old socks but are a popular breakfast dish)' and she went into a tirade about foreign people not appreciating Japanese food. Even when I added that I loved most other kinds of local cuisine, listing sushi and soba as my favourites, she continued anyway. I then said 'I speak English and French,' and she told the students that French was a dialect of English with just a few minor differences. I explained that it was actually an entirely separate language from – you know – a different country, but she refused to believe me. Her final, brilliantly bizarre argument was 'Well, when I went to Ireland, I could understand them.'

I tried to keep a straight face when I said, 'That's because that was Ireland, not France. And they were speaking English.' This still wasn't good enough for her, and she repeated her warped ideas until I had to count to a hundred in order to stop myself committing murder in front of thirty witnesses.

She then told the students to write their own sentences in Japanese, which defeated the object of the activity somewhat, this being an English class. I reiterated my original request, to think of questions to match my sentences, and she told them to think of *other* questions, completely unrelated to anything that I had been trying to teach. In itself this would have merely been annoying, but the real problems arose when some students checked with me what they should be doing. In the interests of consistency I decided the most professional course would be to go with Hasebe's most recent interpretation, but some of the brighter kids noticed the discrepancies between my earlier explanation and the current one, so even more confusion ensued.

It was to become a running theme: a simple activity ruined by Hasebe's need to over-explain in Japanese and then misdirect the students. She didn't have faith in me to make myself understood. More worryingly, she didn't have faith in the students to understand. Before long, I learned her second catchphrase: 'The kids are stupid.'

Conversely, Ms Ikuta was an absolute joy to work alongside. In spite of my misgivings on our first meeting, we soon developed a rapport, and my classes with her felt like a breath of fresh air. She would tell me the general topic of a class, I would design some activities, she would give them the thumbs-up and off we would go. She was great with the kids, quite strict when needed but also very encouraging. Best of all, as far as I was concerned, she insisted the students speak up and use English throughout the class. Again, this may sound obvious, but with Hasebe I was constantly asking students questions only to have her say, 'She doesn't understand,' usually just as the girl was answering. The kids soon realised that they could get through the lesson without making any effort at all because Hasebe would let them off the hook then blame me for daring to ask something as devastatingly tricky as 'How old are you?' It was desperately sad to see students' English deteriorating in front of my eyes. But with Ms Ikuta the emphasis was on participating, and the students really enjoyed the classes. These were the kids that sought me out at lunchtime just because they wanted to practise, something I could never imagine doing with the German Assistant in my own school days.

There was Tomomi, a cute girl with chubby cheeks and winning smile who loved football; Momo chan, with a penchant for digging me in the ribs when I wasn't looking but with a face so innocent that I could never get angry at her; Fujita, the class clown who became so obsessed with the word 'xylophone' that it briefly became his nickname; Kaneda, the teacher's pet who was thirteen going on six and was delighted if I let him press the button on the lift. Adachi and Kimura were the English buffs, annoying their other teachers by doing science or history homework in English and constantly coming out with phrases like 'You'd be a fool to do such a thing' or 'Give me a glass of scotch on the rocks' whenever I least expected. Edo pi was the classic comedy sidekick, overweight and with a constantly worried expression, and he and his friend Haneda bickered endlessly over which comic superhero was better than another. More scarily, there were the precocious third year girls constantly asking about my love-life and soliciting my opinions on their hairstyles and accessories. I became a master at deflecting these enquiries with deft changes of subject:

33

'Garett sensei, what do you think of my new Playboy socks?'

'Nice. What's your favourite pizza topping?'

'Umm… salmon. Do you like Japanese girls?'

'Japanese people are very kind. What's the capital of Australia?'

It was like a tennis match in which they were always serving. Match point had to be when Hina chan shouted my name, I turned around, and she lifted her skirt. Thankfully, she was wearing sports shorts underneath, but my girlish squeal must have echoed across Tokyo Bay. To be on the safe side, I spent the rest of the week with my eyes fixed on the ceiling.

These Are My Children

During a free period, Mr Arakawa, the Vice-Principal, asked me to follow him for a tour of the school. By this time I knew where the main classrooms were. Each year was divided into three classes, the third year rooms on the third floor, second years on the fourth, and first years on the fifth. The lift was out of bounds to students so the logic was that the younger first years could cope with the trek up five flights of stairs more easily than the old and infirm third years. However, I was not yet familiar with the layout of the rest of the school and was glad of a chance to have a wander.

The first floor (Japan follows the sensible American system where the first floor is at ground level) and basement were for the kitchen, admin offices and storage, and the woodchip-filled air betrayed the presence of the craft and technology rooms. The second floor housed the staffroom, Principal's office, meeting rooms and well-stocked library. There was also the nurse's office which was roughly the size of a genuine hospital ward with a row of beds against the wall and curtained-off examination areas. This seemed a bit excessive for a school population of less than three hundred and I felt it positively encouraged students to complain that they were ill, a steady stream of malingerers skiving off lessons to see the lovely nurse, Ms Ono. On the third floor were rooms for science and cooking, plus a traditional tatami mat room resembling a lounge area.

This was for the Japanese culture club where students could arrange flowers and practise the tea ceremony. This kind of flooring, along with the old-style paper windows, needs regular replacement and cleaning and as we went upstairs I discovered a lot of rooms like it, rarely used but obviously expensive to maintain. There was an art gallery, featuring even more of those masterpiece reproductions surrounding a huge matchstick replica of the Eiffel Tower, a martial arts room, an audio-visual room, plus a language laboratory kitted out with headphones, TVs and stereo systems for forty students but usually just used by the four members of English club. An entire orchestra's instruments were scattered around the spacious music room, putting the half-dozen Casio keyboards at my old school to shame. There was even a 'Memorial Hall', a mini-museum of the school's history packed full of sepia-toned photographs and mannequins modelling the uniforms of different eras. I was happy to get out of there, the ghostly atmosphere heightened by the long black drapes lining the walls.

Finally, the *piece de resistance*, as above the massive sports hall was an Olympic-sized swimming pool complete with a retractable domed roof. A particularly nice touch was the canned version of *Greensleeves* that played while the roof whirred open.

Mr Arakawa's proud grin was justifiable as I took in the sights gradually being revealed around us: the modern skyscrapers jutting out of the reclaimed land the school rested upon; the rickety wooden fishermen's houses that lined the river, refusing to be defeated by storms, earthquakes and big business; the misty silhouettes of the Shinjuku and Roppongi entertainment districts; and of course Tokyo Tower, the ugly TV mast I knew from childhood viewings of *Godzilla* but considered by locals the symbol of their awesome city.

I suppose everybody's life is a series of chances, a chain of unplanned incidents only making any sense when it's time to write an obituary, but as I stood next to that pool and looked at the sci-fi cityscape I couldn't help thinking, *How the hell did I end up here?*

We made our way back down to the staffroom, Mr Arakawa gave me a *senbei* rice cracker and we talked a little about our backgrounds. He asked me if I had a family in Japan and I told him I lived with my girlfriend. 'Marriage?' he asked in English. I offered my usual non-committal response to this question, one that was becoming more and more common after five years with Azumi. To be honest, marriage was always something I saw in the distant future, not a tangible goal, so I laughed embarrassedly and asked him about his family. 'No children,' he said, then paused as if to change his mind. He gestured to the classrooms above us. 'These are my children.' I liked Mr Arakawa.

He went back to his work, but as time passed I discovered that he was often quite bored. The Principal stayed in his office, just as I would if I had one that posh, and the rest of the staff were always teaching and preparing lessons. Mr Arakawa led the daily meeting before school, dealt with the occasional visitor and acted as the buffer between the Principal and the rest of the teachers, but most of the time he sat at his desk, sometimes struggling to stay awake and always happy for an excuse to chat. In a funny way, his position was similar to mine. We both existed on the edge of the group with very specific roles but often staving off a sense of worthlessness as we sat helplessly while activity fizzed about us. I hope he appreciated our chats and biscuits because, in those lonely early weeks, I certainly did.

It's a Strange Place

Wednesday afternoons were reserved for teacher meetings, usually in-school but occasionally area-wide. Early in the term, all of the staff travelled the few Metro stops to another of the ward's four junior high schools for a conference followed by smaller subject-specific meetings. The other foreign ALTs were predictably easy to spot: I had been through interview hell alongside Rob, a bright, bearded Australian, and Jim, a huge, bald American who loved to stomp around in Doc Martens and all black attire. Graeme was the veteran with all of six months in the job. A tall, shaggy-haired Englishman, his tight red woolly jumper and exaggerated hand movements gave him the air of a children's TV presenter while his snorts of discontent throughout the admittedly dull opening speeches suggested a personality less suited to that field. This was my first taste of a real meeting in the Japanese school environment but it would turn out to be quite typical, the main topic being the schedule of future meetings. There was a lot of diary-checking and very little of substance but at least we got to meet our colleagues across the area and I could confirm just how unlucky I was to be billeted with Ms Hasebe. The other teachers were a perfectly pleasant bunch who took an interest in the three new ALTs. I accidentally introduced myself as working in the local *senior* high school, a hangover from the misinformation given to me by the agency before my interview, which caused a few laughs at my expense. And one of the interviewers was present, Ms Tsurumi, a woman with the looks and personality of Margaret Thatcher, and the senior teacher in the area. In fairness, she was less ferocious outside the interview room but I would always be a little wary of her suspicious glances and manic questioning of every point raised. I noticed that Graeme wanted to make it very clear that he was the longest-serving ALT, appointing himself the unofficial boss by arranging ALT get-togethers and offering the rest of us pearls of wisdom on life in Japan. He had to leave early but just had time to whisper to me, 'Be careful at your school. It's a strange place.' This was a pretty strange thing to say, just as he was exiting and with no guarantee of when we would meet again, but I guessed it was a reference to Hasebe. Then again, there might be something else to worry about.

I didn't have time to dwell on this mystery as the other JTEs and ALTs headed to a start-of-term party, one of five I had to attend in total. The location of the school and high salary of public teachers in Japan (second only to Sweden, but with significantly lower taxes to pay) meant that these parties were nearly always in high-class, high-priced restaurants in Ginza, the main shopping district of Tokyo where Louis Vuitton and Armani shops sit alongside five-star bistros. My stomach dropped as I walked inside, the *maitre d'* whispering with excessive politeness and leading us to an oak-panelled private room. I hadn't been paid since quitting my previous job three months earlier then travelling around South America. A stomach virus had put me in a hospital on the shores of Lake Titicaca for a few days, further draining my credit card, so *cordon bleu* in the shopping capital of the world was not what I needed. By then, though, it was much too late, so I decided to make the best of the situation by eating as many delicate truffles and tender morsels of veal as I could get my hands on. The staff thoughtfully presented us with an English menu, and it was well above the usual efforts made using translating software – 'pig's anus' and 'chicken cartilage' are best left in Japanese.

Ms Hasebe took an instant and obvious shine to Jim. The big New Yorker was good-natured, incredibly earnest and a bit dim. His character was summed up by the fact that he had lived in Japan for ten years, said nothing but good things about the place, but hadn't bothered to learn any Japanese at all. I've had friends come out to visit for two weeks who picked up more phrases than he had in a decade. As Hasebe tried her luck he was the only person at the table not to twig what was going on. Sadly her clumsy attempts at seduction were limited to insulting his homeland with misjudged banter then telling him he was chubby. This hit a sore nerve and from that day on, whenever I met Jim, he would always drop his 'big muscles' into conversation, a tragic attempt to deny the glaringly obvious, but rather touching nonetheless.

The longer-serving teachers very kindly paid the lion's share of the bill so I could take the train home with a red wine glow and a wallet heavier than I had expected. But, like a scene from a bad melodrama, Graeme's ominous words kept repeating in my head. 'Be careful at your school. It's a strange place.'

Do You Eat Fish Abroad?

The following day, the school held the Sports Test, an annual check-up of the students' height, weight, eyesight, hearing and athleticism, incorporating over twenty different activities throughout the building and taking up an entire morning. Ms Hasebe had told me to come wearing sportswear so I dutifully arrived in my football shorts and T-shirt only to find a staffroom full of teachers in their usual office clothes. I kept hoping that they would all get changed but it never happened and I had to spend a day having students look petrified at the sight of the blond hairs on my bony legs. I thought I should tuck my T-shirt into my shorts as an example to the kids, who were always being badgered to do just that. The style didn't really work, especially when paired with my distinctly unsporty indoor shoes, and I happened to catch sight of myself in the mirror – my metamorphosis into a sad bachelor uncle was complete.

The other departments had held parties the previous evening and a few of the teachers were red-eyed and groggy. I was impressed by their ability to control so many screaming kids while in that condition, with the notable exception of Mr Shimada. As one of the two PE teachers, the Sports Test was an important day for him. Being a fellow newcomer, I imagined he would be keen to show what he could do to his colleagues and bosses. I started the day in the main sports hall with no particular instructions to follow but a notion to look busy by keeping students in line while they waited to do shuttle runs, lift weights and touch their toes. A hundred kids and half the teaching staff milled about energetically. Mr Shimada slumped against a wall, slid to the floor and fell asleep. For a few minutes I wondered if he was OK, but the complete lack of reaction by any student or teacher suggested that they were already accustomed to this kind of behaviour. A line-up for the vault curved around him unblinkingly, as if he were an unpleasant piece of rubbish rather than the sports instructor. Mr Shimada was in so many ways an interesting character. Despite his career educating children in health and fitness, his beer belly spilled out over the elastic of his tracksuit bottoms and his T-shirt bore the debris of yesterday's lunch. He would disappear between classes to puff down a few cigarettes then come back to the staffroom to cough up phlegm in the kitchen sink. He wouldn't wash this down the plughole, but leave it there to solidify and I once had to get a knife to a particularly stubborn chunk. While talking to students he would use his *mimi kaki* (literally 'ear scraper' – a steel stick with a little shovel on the end for scooping out wax, banned in most countries due to the obvious dangers of poking a sharp metal pole in one's ear, but as common as aspirin in Japanese bathroom cabinets). He cut his toenails and shaved his beard at his desk, blew out snot before inspecting it and raided everyone else's coffee supplies. The funny thing was, I kind of liked him. I admired the way he didn't give a damn what anybody – students, teachers, parents, his superiors – thought about him. He just lived his life exactly as he pleased, napping when he felt like it,

44

burping when he felt like it, and collapsing in a drunken daze when he felt like it. The rest of the world could take him or leave him. His bad manners, portly build and love of kids' fantasy novels gave him a childish quality that I found endearing. Even when he sat at the kitchen table, sipping tea while other teachers pitched in to serve up lunch, and only speaking to say 'Ain't no milk' when I gave him his tray, I couldn't help smiling. I tried to work out why he was so appealing despite all his foibles, but it was his foibles that made him so utterly different from anyone I'd met in Japan – and anywhere else for that matter.

I was allowed to try some of the health tests for myself, discovering that I was a decent height for a fourteen-year-old but could do with losing a few pounds. My eyesight was 'better than 20/20' which I thought may qualify me for superhero status until I tried the hand squeeze test. In an epic battle of pressing weights in our fists, I lost to a member of the science club. Chastened, I reverted to the role of spectator. For the students these types of event came as a welcome relief from learning – and there were a lot of them, with culture festivals, sports days, guest speakers, field trips and volunteer activities virtually every week – but for me they were always difficult. Despite asking to be involved, I was never assigned any specific job and I felt that most staff were worried about entrusting me with anything outside the language classroom. While rather insulting, I was more than happy to use this time to catch up on lesson plans, swot up on some Japanese or work on my Master's degree, but Ms Hasebe was intent on having me look busy. I think she felt responsible for the strange foreigner and wanted to make it clear to her colleagues that she had me whipped into shape. Unfortunately, she didn't actually have anything for me to do, so just kept saying, 'Help Ms Ishii.' Ms Ishii, the science teacher who turned pink whenever I came within ten feet of her, was the last person who would want my help, but I had to go through the motions.

'Ms Ishii, can I help you in any way?'

'No, no.'

'Are you sure?'

'Mm.' Struggling for anything else to say, she ran like hell away from this terrifying white man threatening her with offers of assistance. I was left to wander aimlessly, looking faintly absurd as the only adult in sportswear. I counted down the minutes until lunch.

School lunch was one of the highlights of my day. All students received a set meal every day and a nutritionist was employed by the school to carefully balance calories, vitamins and calcium levels. Ms Fukuda sat at the desk opposite mine and was terribly stressed by the difficult task on a very limited budget, but performed miracles in creating varied, high quality meals. Even better, she asked me if I had any requests and, at my behest, cut back on the peanut butter and bananas, just about the only foods I can't stomach. Despite all the space and money available to the school, there was no cafeteria, and the students followed the national norm by eating in their respective classrooms. In true Japanese style, the lunches consisted of about four separate dishes. These were prepared in the on-site kitchen, then wheeled into each classroom to be arranged and served by five or six students from each class. I was deeply impressed by the care taken by most groups to spoon out the food equally, and the patience shown as the students waited for everyone to be ready before they began eating. That was until I saw the third year classes. It was like feeding time in the monkey house and Aesop could write a fable about the kids' attempts to grab more than their fair share and ending up with half of their lunch on the floor. Fourteen and fifteen-year-olds are not the sweetest smelling bunch in any circumstances, but the period right after lunch was a particularly unpleasant time to enter the third years' classroom.

I alternated between eating with the students and eating at the staffroom dining table. The former option was a great way to chat to kids and give them some real English practice. I was always thrilled to find a pupil, who usually kept their head down in class, coming out of their shell in a less formal setting. I was also aware that for many of them, the thought of spending lunch with a teacher was not very enticing, so I tried to keep my visits a novelty. There's nothing more tragic than a teacher trying to be cool, I realised when I visited Graeme's school and saw him playing guitar.

The meals I spent in the staffroom became a lot more pleasant when the part-time teachers started. There were about ten of these occasional staff, each teaching just three or four lessons a day, a couple of times a week and, for some reason, they were a lot friendlier than the majority of full-timers. Perhaps, as with the Vice-Principal, they saw a kindred spirit in me, never being fully integrated into the community, and I looked forward in particular to the days when Ms Kinukawa, Mr Nagizawa and Ms Saguchi were there. Ms Kinukawa had lived in Saudi Arabia and the USA, her husband an engineer in the oil business, and had a decidedly international outlook on life. She was what Japanese people call a 'mood-maker', able to make anyone feel at ease instantly and always the centre of the conversation without ever trying to dominate it. Even the shyest person was soon chatting happily if Ms Kinukawa was at the table. Mr Nagizawa was in his sixties but one of the livelier teachers, always cracking off-colour jokes and telling us about his drinking and gambling exploits. He could sometimes overstep the mark with his deliberately hammed up dirty-old-man act but I always appreciated that he talked to me just as he would anyone else; the fact I was foreign didn't enter into the equation at all. The same couldn't be said for Ms Saguchi, another veteran with the energy of a teenager, who constantly peppered me with questions about *gaikoku*. This term really means 'every country but Japan,' and is a convenient catch-all in a place where many seem to believe that the rest of the world is just one homogenous land, only Japan standing out in its uniqueness. It could become quite grating fielding questions such as, 'Do you eat fish in *gaikoku*?' and, 'How many seasons do you have in *gaikoku*?' but I understood that, poor phrasing aside, she was sincerely interested, as her strident efforts to learn English testified. And at least she always made an effort to be nice to me, along with the other part-timers, and our bilingual lunchtime conversations became something of an institution every Thursday and Friday, the times when I felt human again.

48

Zoe Wannamaker and John Hurt

The official welcome party for new teachers, as well as a farewell for those who had finished at the end of the previous academic year, was held a month into the new term. First, there was a special assembly for all of the school. The recently departed staff made speeches and the students presented them with gifts and flowers in a ceremony I found very moving, even though I didn't know any of them. The requisite harshness of work life in Japan meant that most didn't know that they were being transferred until a few weeks earlier and were discouraged from discussing their departures with the students. Therefore this ceremony was the only chance to say goodbye, causing tears aplenty. In spite of a reputation for being reserved and hiding emotion, the Japanese have an immense capacity for crying. Bad news is met with a bawl, good news with a smiling sob. New movies are often advertised not by images from the film itself but by video footage of the audience weeping. It's little wonder that game centres and restaurants promote themselves by handing out free packets of tissues at train stations, and I was glad to have a few of these in my pocket as the students broke down one by one.

Afterwards, the kids went home and the teachers made their way to a hotel, once again in Ginza, for a buffet party. I was stuck next to Hasebe, who brazenly mistranslated everything I said to the other teachers at the table, even when I said them in Japanese. She did her best to paint me as the naïve foreigner. She asked if I liked *sake*, I said yes, and she told everyone that I couldn't drink it. She asked about my favourite places in Japan, I listed a few, and she reported that I hadn't travelled much so didn't know anywhere but Tokyo. I tried to correct her but had to tread a fine line between getting my point across and getting wound up at her senseless, compulsive lies. I again planned to devour as much posh food as possible but the five thirty start meant that I wasn't very hungry, so I just devoured the beer instead. From the moment the party began various guests were invited by Mr Kubo, the history teacher with a fondness for Italian wines, to make speeches. These are a common occurrence at most kinds of party and ceremony though I'm not precisely sure why. The person making the speech is under pressure to try and come up with something that hasn't already been said; the audience is prevented from any real conversation as they have to make a show of listening; in reality, nobody pays attention because they're too busy eating, drinking and – in true Japanese style, for I've never known a people so predisposed to public napping – falling asleep. As with so much in this very conservative culture, speeches were another ritual to be observed simply because they had always had them, practicality and enjoyment taking a backseat. The only plus point for me was that Ms Hasebe assured me that I wouldn't have to take the stage. 'It's only for proper teachers,' she informed me sweetly. Once again, she was wrong.

'We have time for one more speech,' Mr Kubo announced, to the noise of uncomfortable shuffling all round. 'Garett sensei!'

'Bugger,' I muttered.

Being the foreigner in the ranks, I had been roundly ignored by most teachers in those first few weeks, but the chance to hear me make a speech filled the room with expectation. The clatter of cutlery, the murmur of quiet asides, and the snoring, all came to a sudden halt as I made the long walk to the microphone. I hastily tried to construct some decent sentences in my alcohol-swirling head. One of the many stumbling blocks to learning Japanese is its many levels of politeness. Having picked it up primarily from my girlfriend and mates, I was aware that my language was casual verging on impolite, something that wouldn't do in a formal situation such as this. The sudden need to stand up after five large bottles of Asahi and the adrenalin rush caused by Mr Kubo's surprise request meant that the blood rushed to my face, my voice stammered and I could only talk in platitudes:

'I'm very pleased to be here. It's been a wonderful party. I hope we can all work hard together and have a productive year.'

There were a few nods of encouragement, possibly even gratitude, and I started warming to the crowd. 'I know that many foreign teachers come and only teach English. But I hope I can be more than just an ALT. I want to belong to the team, I want to really contribute to the community.' Roars of approval all round and I could retire to my seat with a glow in my heart as I noticed a sudden change in everyone's expressions towards me. The Principal came over and patted me on the back. He called me Garett. I'd won them over.

Most office parties here start with the more formal do and are then followed by second, third, and, for the hard core, fourth parties, standards of politeness gradually deteriorating. About half of the group decided to go on to an *izakaya*, the nearest equivalent to a British pub but where a ready supply of food is always available. Mr Kubo had until now largely ignored me, but following a few glasses of chianti and a jug of *sake*, he was my new best friend. It transpired that he was something of an Anglophile, particularly keen on Andrew Lloyd Webber and Maggie Smith, and we had quite an in-depth conversation on the topic of British theatre. He had seen some taped performances of the Royal Shakespeare Company on NHK, the public broadcaster, and drilled me for extra information on the cast. I'm no Shakespeare buff but thanks to my love of *Star Wars* and *Harry Potter*, I knew many of the actors he admired and I could speak quite knowledgeably on the subject. I wasn't to know then that the whole half-hour dialogue would become a staple of every work party, Mr Kubo forgetting our previous chat and waxing just as lyrically each time about Zoe Wannamaker and John Hurt. I didn't complain as Mr Kubo was the *de facto* leader of the team who appeared to wield more power in the day-to-day running of the school than the Principal or Vice-Principal. He was someone I wanted on my side.

Later we went on to that most Japanese of entertainments, karaoke. Whenever I'd tried – or, more likely, been forced into – karaoke at home, I had always despised it. A city centre bar packed with drunken hecklers was never a great venue for my talents. But in

Japan groups can rent small rooms just for their own party and, after a couple of colleagues make fools of themselves, it becomes perfectly natural to belt out Elvis at the top of your lungs. Between rounds of beer, *shochu* and *sake* – ordered through the handy intercom and delivered by discreet waiters who barely raise an eyebrow, even at my show-stopping rendition of *Little Mermaid* favourites – the mostly male contingent sang their hearts out. After my workmates' encouragement, I even performed the puzzling but traditional *salaryman* act of tying my necktie around my head, ninja-style, and Mr Arakawa, the Vice-Principal, insisted on paying my bill.

Before I knew it, we had to run to the station. This is one of the more annoying aspects of Tokyo life, and it still surprises me that such a twenty-four-hour city doesn't have any night trains or buses. There's a mad panic every midnight as the drunken hordes fight it out for a place on the last train and, no matter your condition, it isn't pleasant. On my first ever experience of the journey, a university student vomited on the sliding doors inside the carriage, so at each stop his gastric juices would squeegee along the Perspex and onto the floor. One poor businessman stepped in it, his feet flew up in the air, cartoon-style, and he landed in the slimy puddle. On this occasion, though, I had the buzz of free drink to keep me company, as well as the certainty that my relationship with the rest of the school staff had turned a corner. From now on, everything would be better.

That Class Is Pretty Stupid

The weekend was one long hangover, but by Monday I was fully recovered and happy to see a perfect spring sky. After the morning train squeeze and canned coffee, I'd come to particularly enjoy the view from the bridge I had walked over so full of trepidation on that rainy first day. When the air was clear, or as clear as it ever could be in Tokyo, the shimmering domes of Odaiba – yet another area of reclaimed land covered in newly-built shops and offices – were a beautiful sight, and the faint aroma of sea air made me think of holidays. They were a long way off yet, but my sense of optimism couldn't be diminished. I had finally made friends with the other teachers and they were sure to embrace me into their previously closed community.

I entered the staffroom full of cheerful hellos and thanks for a great party. In return I got exactly the same response I had always received: a half-smile, a mumble or two of recognition and a distinct lack of warmth. Initially I wondered if some people felt embarrassed by their drunken behaviour, but when the same pattern was repeated after every party throughout the year I deduced that most of my colleagues simply compartmentalised their lives in such a way that a heartfelt chat and karaoke duet on a Friday night had no bearing at all on any professional relationship. Frankly, I found this cold and a bit sad because the hushed, scholarly atmosphere in the staffroom would have been brightened by a bit more friendliness, but ultimately I just had to grudgingly accept it, and wait for Thursday when the part-time teachers would rescue me with their lunchtime chat.

My springtime energy was slowly sucked out of me by my classes with Ms Hasebe. Her only goal was to make it to the end of each lesson, to fill those fifty minutes one way or another. She wasn't interested in inspiring the students or encouraging English communication. She just wanted to get by. As one of the world's leading experts in the field of getting by, I could empathise, but even I draw the line at shortchanging children's education. I constantly created activities that I hoped would get the students using the language for more than just grammar tests, but Hasebe was reluctant to try anything that required any classroom management on our parts. Even when she agreed beforehand to do a speaking activity, she would change her mind halfway through the lesson, without informing me, then try and adapt the game into a writing exercise, usually with embarrassing results. Then, when it didn't work because she hadn't thought things through as she butchered my idea, she blamed it on my activity. To add to my woes, she also interrupted me whenever I was teaching, clearly trying to remind the students that I was the assistant and she was the boss. Everything I said would be cut short by her questioning what I was doing, very loudly so that the students presumed I must have erred, and I was continuously biting my tongue during lessons.

For someone so comically half-witted it was frustrating but

amusing to see her think everyone else was the idiot. She explained things to me in weirdly minute detail, even when I indicated my understanding.

'So, Garett, today we're going to do that numbers worksheet with the first years.'

'OK.'

'You know, numbers.'

'Got it. I made that worksheet.'

'One, two, three. Numbers.'

'Yes, numbers.'

'You know, numbers. Four, five, six.'

'OK!'

'Seven, eight. Numbers.'

The only bonus was that sarcasm was completely lost on her. 'Will you be requiring nine and ten, too? I know the full range.'

'Umm… Yeah, that class is pretty stupid but I think they can manage it.'

This was small consolation, though, as I found myself fuming every day, a tight pain in my stomach increasing as the term went on. And my girlfriend Azumi felt the stress almost as much as me. Every night I went home and needed to let out all the pent-up irritation, tale after tale of Hasebe's stupidity, rudeness and attempts to humiliate me. Azumi listened patiently and sympathetically, always able to choose the perfect words of comfort or simply nod with understanding at just the right time, and my feelings for her grew even stronger. For that, if nothing else, I can thank Ms Hasebe.

Perhaps my annoyance was heightened by my good fortune at also working with Ms Ikuta. The contrast between the two was profound as Ms Ikuta insisted on a well-behaved class fully participating in English-speaking exercises, while Ms Hasebe meekly allowed the students to do as they pleased – making paper planes, writing letters to one another, shouting while the teachers were giving vital instructions – just as long as they didn't cause *too* much trouble. After a lesson teaching Ms Ikuta's open-faced, invigorated students, it was very hard to adapt to the *Lord of the Flies* re-enactments in Hasebe's classes. Even more emasculating was the fact that my agency forbade me to discipline the kids in any way. Of course the reality of the situation meant that I was forced to raise my voice at times (I'd never imagined I would have to be the hard-arse teacher!) but Ms Hasebe would even stop me doing that, insisting that every student had some kind of behavioural problem and therefore should never be told off. The result was that her classes were dominated by a few bad kids, and the majority had no opportunity to learn.

My previous stereotyped view of Japanese schools had been of a strict, no-nonsense approach where the teachers ruled with an iron fist and the occasional beating. While I don't condone violence as a form of punishment, I was surprised to see a complete lack of any penalty for misbehaviour. There were no detentions, no extra homework – in fact, very little homework at all – and no trips to the Principal's office. The worst an errant student would face was Mr Kubo yelling. Admittedly, this was a scary sight, but it began to lose its effect after a few dozen outings, and the really bad kids even appeared to enjoy that – a very public announcement of their acts of rebellion for children who were looking for attention in the first place.

Each teacher in the school was allocated a particular year to look after and the group overseeing the third years was, sadly, very weak. Aside from Mr Kubo and his tantrums, they were all competing to be the kindest, most popular teacher, and the students duly ran wild. Their floor was like a war zone, and if I didn't have to enter it a couple of times a day alongside Hasebe, it would have been hilarious. It reminded me of those American high school comedies where absolute hell was breaking out all around but with no-one paying any heed. Full-scale wrestling matches took place alongside food fights; nerdy kids were stuffed in cupboards; obscene graffiti was chalked on the wall, but nobody cared. It seemed nobody could – or wanted to – do anything about it.

In contrast, the teachers for the other grades, especially the second year to which Ms Ikuta belonged, worked hard to create and maintain a good atmosphere where students were aware of the boundaries but could really thrive. Most importantly, the kids respected themselves and each other, a quality decidedly lacking among many egocentric third years, much to the shame of themselves and their teachers.

It came as a relief to get a break from Hasebe's put-downs and the third years' institutionalised unpleasantness – at least in the classroom – as everything stopped for Sports Day.

Heil Hitler

Sports Day has far greater significance in Japanese schools than in the West and is one of the highlights of the calendar for staff, students and parents. Lessons were cancelled almost in their entirety for the two weeks prior to the day itself as every teacher organised practice sessions, and every student shed blood, sweat and tears in the sweltering June heat. Club activities, too, were called off to be replaced by further training drills in which the strongest were chosen to compete in the main events and the weakest were left face-down in the dust of the school sports ground. And what were these events, the cause of so much struggle, pain and bitterness? Three-legged runs, egg and spoon races and *Rawhide* (where a girl in a cowboy hat is carried by two classmates and tries to lasso a bucket). There was something both endearing and disturbing about teenagers, teetering on the brink of adulthood, putting so much effort into *It's a Knockout* comedy games, even more so the teachers' distraught reactions when Edo pi and Haneda still couldn't perform a star jump properly.

As with the earlier Sports Test, and every other special event throughout the year, I was kept very much on the sidelines, the responsibility of blowing a starter's whistle or holding a finish-line tape considered too complex for me to handle. And, once again, I had Ms Hasebe saying things like, 'Go and help over there,' when there was blatantly nothing to be done, so that I ended up having to pretend to look busy – always a lot harder than *being* busy – just to stop her from giving me another empty instruction.

As well as the races themselves, there were numerous other presentations and displays to open and close the games. I particularly enjoyed marching practice – three hundred kids stomping in time to *National Velvet*, the dust of the school yard puffing up in clouds around them – and was again reminded of the military. Despite having no official army, Japan needn't worry about being invaded by North Korea or Russia; they just have to send out the junior high school kids. (I'd happily have volunteered my third years for the first wave.) On top of this marching, there were intricate dances and energetic gymnastics displays, the human pyramid a bloodbath waiting to happen and therefore eminently watchable. The sports field was apparently designed by a psychopath to be as painful as possible to fall on – a layer of uneven gravel on concrete – so the students became well used to suffering. It looked like the opening scene of *Saving Private Ryan* as bodies lay prostrate and the ground ran red with blood, Ms Ono, the school nurse, struggling manfully to reach the fallen with nothing but a first aid box and a towel. Then, as the students lined up for speeches and pep talks from the Principal, their kit muddy and bloody, some kids fainting in the baking heat of that uncovered yard, I thought of another war film: *The Bridge on the River Kwai*. I half-expected a belligerent Alec Guinness to plead the Geneva Convention as vultures circled overhead. My sense of uselessness was worsened by the harshness of the sun, and outdoor drills seemed to be timed for the moments when no shade protected us – an impressive achievement in a school surrounded by fifty-storey skyscrapers.

The staffroom had a balcony which overlooked the sports ground so occasionally I was able to sneak away and enjoy the spectacle from a distance. Mr Nagizawa and I sipped iced tea together, pausing intermittently to check on the progress of the marching drills and chuckling at the suspiciously fascist salute the class leaders gave the Principal. 'Heil Hitler,' Mr Nagizawa deadpanned.

One of the higher points of Sports Day preparation was the chance to get better acquainted with Seiko chan. Special schools for disabled children do exist in Japan but entry is optional and parents are allowed to send their child to a regular school if they wish. My initial feeling on seeing Seiko – profoundly disabled, physically and mentally, and unable to speak or walk – was that she would be better served in a school designed to meet her requirements. I felt that her parents were trying to dodge the issue of her special needs, preferring to pretend that she was a regular, fully-functioning member of society when, sadly, she wasn't. By joining the usual classes she would be unable to get the support she needed, and her classmates would suffer from the obvious distraction as her careworkers gave her separate activities while the main lessons went on. But that was before I got to know Seiko and her mother. Her parents were all too aware of her situation and constantly grateful to the teachers for the extra care they took with their daughter. They also knew that for the rest of her life, maybe seventy or eighty years, Seiko would be in special schools, special hospitals, special homes, and they just wanted her to gain a taste of 'normal life' while she still had the chance. I felt humbled, embarrassed by my earlier judgements. These were the people who knew Seiko better than anyone, the people who would devote their entire selves to her welfare, so it was only right that they were able to choose the best course for her.

Seiko was attended to by two part-time support staff, Mika and Yoshiko, who kept her constantly amused with their games and good humour, and Seiko clearly enjoyed her school life. Although unable to participate in any Sports Day events, she was fully involved in the ceremonies surrounding it, and was an ever-present at the practice sessions, Mika and Yoshiko keeping her occupied with balloons and ribbons representing her team. As I struggled to find things to do, it was a welcome break to join this trio as they made pom-poms and confetti and generally had fun. Seiko was an unbelievable flirt, constantly holding hands with any males in the vicinity, then playing two off against each other by alternating her affections. Mr Shimada and I became great rivals. Seiko suffered from eczema and would repeatedly employ me as her neck-scratcher, grabbing my hand and pulling it into the correct position. At least I was a use to someone in those long hot days.

He Said I Was Going Bald

The school was split into three teams for Sports Day – red, yellow and blue – and the afternoons leading up to it were taken up with separate practices for the group presentations. They each arranged a song based upon recent J-Pop offerings but with lyrics altered to extol the virtues of their team and – slightly cringingly – their captain, always a boy and usually the biggest or most popular. This was accompanied by a dance choreographed by the motherly third year girls and carried out with earnest determination by even the most rebellious kids. The concerted effort was rather sweet, but I also felt frustrated that this kind of enthusiasm couldn't be channelled into more worthwhile causes. Still, I could appreciate the value to team-building, any group ethic severely lacking in regular classes, and I did enjoy the school bully's effete twirl as his gymnastics ribbon circled around him.

As these separate practices took place I walked around the building, helping where I could, but mostly keen to see the dances and flag displays. I took the lift to the fifth floor where I knew the yellow team was deep in rehearsal. I arrived to find no teachers but a violent scrap going on between some first year boys. It appeared that three of them were attacking Imura, a small, intelligent but rather odd boy. I shouted at them to leave him alone, they backed off, and Imura went crazy. He lashed out at anyone nearby – friends, classmates, complete strangers – his mouth foaming and eyes white with anger. Like Warner Brothers' Tasmanian Devil he cut a swathe through the crowd, his fists and feet flying everywhere.

'What's going on?' I shouted above the screams and crunch of bones. Wakana, one of the more sensible third year girls, tried to explain but Imura latched onto her leg and began gnawing at it. My agency's no-discipline rule wasn't much use when I was the only teacher present and a boy was looking to cannibalise anybody who happened to cross his path, so I pulled him off Wakana's thigh and wrapped my arms tight around him. He was a feisty little bugger, wriggling free so I had to grab him again, then biting my arm and digging his jagged fingernails into my side. I needed back-up.

Wakana ran to find another member of staff and, fortunately, it was Ms Ikuta (Ms Hasebe would probably have told me to put him down and allow him to pulverise a few classmates because 'He has problems'). She took his feet and I kept hold of his arms and body, my main concern being his gnashing teeth edging towards my neck. The three boys he had been fighting initially tried to join in but I advised them that further poking and shouting at him would not be the best course of action, and Ms Ikuta and I managed to drag him into the lift. He was still hissing and growling, still clawing at my skin and kicking Ms Ikuta's arms, but we finally got him to the empty library and he began to calm down. I've never seen a human being look so animalistic, his expression now one of a cornered dog, looking around for an escape route but realising he was beaten. We tried to soothe him, a tricky thing to do as he occasionally yapped and bared his teeth between seething breaths. At last he cooled off enough to ask him what was wrong.

'Furukawa said I was going bald.'

'Oh, dear. Well, you're definitely not going bald. What else did he say?'

'Nothing.'

'Did he attack you? Did he hurt you?'

'No.'

'Did he threaten you?'

'No.'

'So why did you act the way you did?'

'He said I was going bald.'

Twelve is an interesting age. Some children are well on their way to puberty and maturity while others, such as Imura, retain the obsessive nature of the infant, hyper-sensitive to criticism and desperate for positive attention. He never apologised for his disturbing, violent outburst, and never showed signs of doing it again. A day later he was laughing and joking with the same boys he had been ready to murder. The only change I detected was that his previous reserve whenever I'd approached him was replaced with something verging on affection. His efforts in English class doubled and he scolded any student who dared speak out of line while I was teaching. Most importantly, I'm glad to say, he still has a full head of hair.

On the Friday before Sports Day, the staff had to erect tarpaulin canopies to shade the expected crowd. The students would have to sit in the sun, this whole event a lesson in character-building, but at least they got to help us snap rusting metal poles into place and hammer in bolts with mallets and drills. Japan is obviously a first world, highly-developed country, but its attitude to health and safety issues is very loose. Practicality comes first, as paraffin lamps are left to burn in the middle of tightly-packed restaurants, frayed electric wires trail across shop floors, and schoolchildren are given power tools to play with. I kind of liked it, and thankfully on this occasion there were no injuries any more serious than those already happening out on the track.

The marquees were soon up, the tannoy system was loud and clear, and I discovered the reason for the gravelly yard: blood and severed body parts could be quickly raked under the dirt, much like a sawdust floor in a Wild West saloon, leaving the illusion of cleanliness. The school nurse issued a leaflet in which students were given final instructions to rest well and remember to eat a hearty breakfast, a quaintly patronising message considering the carnage they were facing. Sunday was the big day.

A Lasso in the Eye

As a rule, Sports Days in Japan are held in autumn when the weather is pleasantly mild and rainfall is least likely. I don't know why my school chose to have theirs in June. If the sun and humidity weren't sapping every ounce of energy out of the students and spectators, then the rainy season was unleashing its fury. After two weeks of the former, the odds favoured a storm, and I woke up to a black sky and oppressive air.

It being a Sunday the train was much less crowded than usual and I enjoyed the luxury of being able to get a seat on the Sobu line, but with half an eye on the streaks of rain hitting the windows. At Ryogoku I needed my umbrella for the walk between stations and the same spitting drizzle was falling as I crossed the river next to the school. The contingency plan was to postpone Sports Day until Tuesday and have regular lessons instead, so I passed through the gate and readied myself for a day teaching classes of disappointed and disinterested students. Inside, the sight of kids in their PE kit and teachers rushing around busily told me otherwise: Sports Day was on.

The staffroom reminded me of Mission Control at launch time, meetings next to meetings with Mr Arakawa shouting over the top and weather charts jumping off the printer. Everything pointed to more rain, but nobody wanted to make the final call and cancel. The fact that the Meteorological Society predicted a ninety percent chance of precipitation the entire day was not enough to dissuade us; that left a ten percent chance of good weather, after all. The glimmer of sunlight between blankets of dark cloud was just enough to convince Mr Arakawa to say 'Carry on' as if willpower alone would stave off the inevitable. The students went outside and the last-minute preparations began.

I was always impressed by the school band, and never more so than on that dreary morning when they blasted out fanfares and show tunes to ward off the rain and lift the spirits of the sparse crowd (most parents had presumed, too, that the event would be cancelled). What had looked scarily similar to a forced death march during the week was now carried out by the students with gusto and precision; speeches were made and Nazi salutes delivered in perfect time and the children took their positions for the warm-up. This ritual is observed before almost every PE class in every school in Japan: a jaunty 1940s tune rang out over the loudspeakers and the students and teachers knew each move in a sequence of stretches working every part of the body for five minutes. Before the practices I had been talking to Seiko and her helpers or running away from Ms Hasebe, so I hadn't studied the choreography. Rather arrogantly I had thought of it as something for the kids to do and me to snigger at, but they had the last laugh. All the teachers were called forward to perform the dance as a guide to the students and, as I happened to be next to the Principal at the time, I couldn't find a suitable hiding place. The familiar opening bars played and, miraculously, I remembered the moves. I pulled my arms into a theatrical stretch above my head. Sadly, no-one else did, and as time went on I discovered that I *did* know every move – just not in the right order. This was the second time I'd met most of the parents and, just like at the start-of-term ceremony, I made an idiot of myself. When the music stopped I skulked into a corner and cursed the rain for not falling.

The games themselves ran smoothly, with minimal blood and only one hospitalisation (a lasso in the eye during *Rawhide* causing temporary blindness). I managed to make myself useful by lugging crash mats around and pretending to be ready to catch any falling third years at the human pyramid. My mood was improving.

Next was the assault course, as students raced along beams, under hurdles, over vaults and through nets. Almost imperceptibly, the moist air turned into tiny droplets and these joined to make a misty drizzle. Still we continued, hoping that it was a passing cloudburst, and the kids slid along the wet wooden beam and splashed through slowly expanding puddles. I was supervising the forward roll over the big PVC mat, employing a team of first years to help me towel down the surface after one girl slid off the end, her neck and back scraping through the wet gravel for a good ten yards afterwards. The towels soon became sodden and useless but my pleas to end the misery went unheeded. Finally, a boy had a nasty accident on the beam, almost certainly preventing him from being a father in future years, and the children were told to go inside.

The parents huddled under the marquee, and the teachers milled about in a hectic illusion of activity when, in reality, all we could do was wait and hope. There followed another series of shouted meetings and another round of calls to various agencies in the hope that one of them might say the weather would improve. A look out of the window was a clear indicator otherwise. Thunder boomed and the drizzle gained weight, soon reminiscent of rain I'd only before seen in Florida when summer afternoons would be punctured by half an hour of end-of-the-world torrents; only this day it went on and on. But even this wasn't enough and the kids were kept in their classrooms while their teachers dithered over a blatantly obvious choice. As it wasn't yet midday, it was decided to wait until lunchtime, and the equipment was left to soak, along with the students' classroom chairs that they had taken outside but forgotten to bring in.

An hour passed before Sports Day was officially cancelled. Only then did it occur to anyone to try and save the furniture that had been left out to rot. After two weeks of being refused every time I offered to assist anyone, I was finally given something to do: I was told to go outside and cover the chairs with plastic sheets. Mr Shimada joined me in the ridiculous task. It was obviously too late as the wood was already completely saturated and by covering them we would only trap the damp inside for the next two days. We were risking our lives in running across the huge open ground as lightning cracked about us, and the rain flooded our summer clothes. I was more than a little peeved as we carried out the pointless mission. The wind blew the massive plastic sheets in the air and we fought to tuck the edges under the outlying chair legs. My t-shirt was clinging to

72

my body, suffocating me, and my socks were squelching in my shoes. In my angry state it was easy to become cynical about the famous Japanese work ethic. There's no doubt that people do work much longer hours than those in the West, and the economic miracle of the post-war years is a tribute to that. But so much of it, both in this job and in the society as a whole, is done simply for the sake of looking busy, with very little direction. That's why there was so much activity when I arrived at the start of the day but no-one willing to take responsibility. It's also why a workman is made to stand next to a construction site all day and tell passersby not to climb over the fluorescent orange fence and fall into that big black hole; or why a shop that could easily be run by two people will employ five members of staff but insist they each work twelve-hour shifts, despite only being paid for eight – if their shifts were staggered the workers would be fresher, less bored and more productive but it's just *the done thing* to power through, regardless of results.

I get annoyed when I find myself trying to graft my own ideals onto a different culture's but, as the water stung my eyes, my shorts slipped off my hips and the plastic sheet just refused to stay in place, I think I could be forgiven for wishing a bit of common sense would prevail over the blinkered desire not to be perceived lazy.

We eventually completed our ordeal and trudged back inside to be blasted by the ice-cold air conditioner. Right on cue, the sky cleared and the sun returned. I shivered at my desk and the students' chairs slowly rotted. The plastic sheets were dry within the hour.

You're a Waste of Space

A staff party had been planned for the evening of Sports Day as reward for everyone's efforts. It had initially been arranged that the party would be cancelled if the games weren't completed but, again, no-one wished to be the bearer of that message so it went ahead regardless. The pats on the back for a job well done were half-hearted – we still had most of the activities to complete the following Tuesday – and the mood was consolatory rather than celebratory as we walked to the *izakaya*.

We settled down on the *tatami* floor and cushions – no chairs – and I was glad to be next to the wall so that I could lean against something; even after four years of practice I still struggled to hold a *seiza* kneel or cross-legged squat for more than a few minutes. Ms Maki, a just-appointed part-time English teacher, sat next to me. For reasons I never discovered, she had been hired a few weeks into the school term and in the chaos of Sports Day training we had barely had the chance to exchange two words. However, her wide smile and her look of amused confusion whenever Ms Hasebe gave another garbled order made me sense that she would become an ally. Beforehand she had worked in a private senior high school and I found it hard to picture her surrounded by lanky eighteen-year-old boys when she was so petite and – at twenty-five – so young for a teacher; I would often confuse her for a student whenever she wore navy, our school uniform's colour. She asked me about the other English teachers and I didn't think it would be fair to prejudice her by letting loose on Ms Hasebe, so I kept my comments fairly neutral on the subject. She, too, was diplomatic as she gave her impressions, but before long we let our guards down and it was thanks to Ms Maki that I was able to cope with Hasebe as long as I did. I always suspected that Ms Ikuta had her doubts about Hasebe but she was far too professional to discuss the issue with me, her subordinate. Ms Maki, however, as a part-timer, could be more open and it was hugely refreshing to be able to have a good whinge with a fellow victim. If anything, Ms Maki's arrival made Ms Hasebe even more unbearable as she tried to stamp her authority on the expanding English department. Her method of doing so was to criticise anything the other teachers did – a cowardly act as she knew that I, the assistant, had no comeback without risking my job – but the load felt a great deal lighter now that I could share it with Ms Maki. And my daily gripe to Azumi could be shortened by twenty minutes.

The evening was warm and relaxing after such a stressful day and Ms Maki played the role of hostess to perfection. It's an endearing trait of the Japanese that they will serve everyone else before themselves, sometimes to the point of excess as the entire group waits for someone else to take the first piece of sashimi or first swig of beer. Ms Maki insisted on dishing out the communal food for me and constantly topping up my beer glass. At times this can feel a bit cloying, the over-formality getting in the way of relaxed, casual chat, but in this case it felt nice to be pampered – the risk of trench foot still a real possibility in my soggy socks.

The usual toasts and speeches were made, to our hard work (if only half-completed) and to the new faces (Ms Maki was joined by new part-timers in mathematics and Japanese). The food and drink was almost finished and people were thinking about going home. As I talked to Ms Maki, I happened to catch snatches of a drunken conversation between Mr Arakawa, the Vice-Principal, and Mr Shimada, the porcine PE teacher. Mr Arakawa, ever the gentleman, was doing his best to keep Mr Shimada's voice down: 'You're saying too much now. Let's just enjoy the party.' But the portly sports instructor wouldn't be stopped.

'This school's terrible. I'm putting in for a transfer. Nobody cares about sport here and there's no kind of community. Nobody cares.'

He went on in this vein, the classic comedy lush, as the Vice-Principal tried to save him from himself. I actually agreed with some of what Mr Shimada said but I also realised that a party wasn't the best time to say it, especially with Mr Kubo in earshot. The veteran history teacher, the longest serving and most intimidating teacher in the school, Mr Kubo was even more frightening after a few cups of *shochu*, beer and wine (he always was one to mix his drinks). If he wasn't sleeping off the drink or asking for my opinions on the relative merits of *Miss Saigon* and *Cats*, he was busting for a fight. Now he had one. As with most of his very frequent tantrums, this one started quietly. First he just muttered to himself, then to those adjacent and, finally, to the whole gathering.

77

'Shimada goes on about people caring... What about him? He spent most of the day sitting in the kitchen drinking tea! He hardly did anything during all the rehearsals, he comes in late and never helps out. He just sleeps and eats. And he's meant to be the PE teacher!'

As Mr Kubo became more excited, he rose to his feet. With the rest of us still sitting on the floor he towered above us and the low long table. Mr Shimada tried his best to look nonchalant, waving his hand dismissively but probably regretting his ill-timed comments, and Kubo's rant gained momentum.

'You're a waste of space! You're no teacher! I hope you do get a transfer! Then we'll be rid of you!'

I was in partial agreement with him too, although, in fairness, Mr Shimada had been the one to join me in my battle with the wet chairs and plastic sheets. Kubo leaned over the table and I had to grab the tail of his jacket to prevent him from toppling on top of the empty glasses and scraps of uneaten salad. He tried to get across the table to Shimada, so Mr Nakamura and I had to keep hold of his suit, his body dangling at a forty-five-degree angle over the table. Mr Arakawa deserved the Nobel Prize for his peacemaking skills, clearly very unhappy with Shimada's comments but also keen to avoid the scandal of his teachers being arrested for brawling in the middle of a crowded restaurant, and right in the centre of the school's catchment area.

Mr Kubo's fury receded enough for us to let go of him and he sat back down, hissing with impotent anger. Mr Shimada sensibly decided to go home. The party was over.

I walked to the station feeling quite shocked by the whole incident. I had seen a few of Mr Kubo's outbursts before, where he growled at everyone in sight then chucked whatever happened to be in his hand as hard as he could. In the lead up to Sports Day he'd had one of these, throwing a stack of CD cases against the wall, causing the discs to spill out of the cracked casing; this got him even more riled so he picked the pile up and pitched it at the swing-top dustbin. The lid of the bin broke, one of cases smashed into his favourite coffee mug, and the whole staff ducked for cover as he picked up his laptop computer and raised it over his head. He finally saw sense and dropped it heavily back onto his desk – it's only taxpayers' money after all – then rashed and snashed like Mutley while the rest of us stifled our nervous laughter. But on this occasion in the *izakaya* his malice was aimed at an individual, and that made it a lot more terrifying.

Where the Hell Are You?

Feeling depressed, and with a few drinks already inside me, I thought it would be a good idea to have a few more. I texted my friend Neil, a former colleague who had returned home to Ireland but was now in Tokyo on business, and I went to meet him near his hotel.

Shibuya is one of the major entertainment centres of Tokyo, a seething mass of young people. Hachiko Crossing in front of the station is said to be the busiest pedestrian intersection in the world, hundreds of people at a time waiting for the green light at each of the five crossing points. When the lights flash the hordes clash in the middle like warriors in *Braveheart*, until each person can force a way through to their destination – usually a bar, night club or clothes shop.

I had arranged to meet Neil just next to the crossing, at the statue of Hachiko, a dog who faithfully followed his master to the station every day, continuing even after the man had died. This has become the main meeting point in Shibuya and there are always hundreds of people waiting there, glancing furtively at watches and phones, and checking their clothes and hair before their dates arrive. Many of these flock to the area in the latest outrageous fashions, dyed hair and wacky make-up at odds with mainstream society. My date had fair hair, at least; he was also six-foot tall and wearing an Ireland rugby shirt.

We went to a bar and Neil gladly helped me drown my sorrows. We talked a lot about old times in the conversation school up in Tochigi prefecture, and about his fiancée Maire's pregnancy. Neil and Maire had come to Japan together and got engaged on Mt Fuji, which was incredibly romantic and incredibly cold. I was thrilled for their happiness but privately concerned that I was being further left behind as everyone around me seemed to be growing up. So I changed the subject to football.

We went to another bar and sank more beers, the walls of neon around us spinning and blurring. I'm a big fan of Japanese beer, especially in summer, as it's refreshingly easy-to-drink and not nearly as heavy as British ale. The problem is that I can't judge the amount. While with creamy beers back home I begin to slow down as my stomach fills up, Asahi or Kirin feels as light after the tenth glass as the first – and due to its fizziness and higher alcohol content, it has a kick in it similar to tequila. One minute I was lucid, if a bit chatty; the next I was thoroughly hammered.

Neil went back to his hotel and I ran to catch the last train. I waited on the platform a few minutes, pleasantly surprised that it was so quiet and I'd be able to get a seat on the carriage. A station guard approached me cautiously. 'The trains have finished for the night,' he told me, bowing with shame, as if it were his fault. The sensible course of action would have been to phone Neil and kip on his hotel floor; or find a capsule hotel, where for very reasonable prices I could sleep in a coffin-like room with just enough space for my narrow mattress and an overhead TV. Unfortunately, I was in no state for sensible courses of action, so I chose to find another bar and drink my way through till the trains started again in the morning. I wandered some backstreets, no doubt meandering carelessly across the road, and stumbled upon a little 'shot bar' specialising in whisky and vodka. I only remember snatches: the cheerful barman, the tanginess of bourbon and Coke, the equally drunk old man playing darts and trying to coax me into a match – a recipe for disaster if ever there was, but one I managed to turn down.

Drunk-logic at its best, I thought that I shouldn't disturb Azumi by calling or texting as she had work the next day (my school was closed in lieu of the Sunday Sports Day), so I spent the next four hours slowly pickling myself in spirits, my phone stored safely in my bag.

I have a vague memory of crawling back to the station, the morning daylight always a nasty shock on these occasions. I remember getting onto a train and employing my bag as a pillow as I settled into the soft velour seat. Then I was happy to close my eyes as the carriage filled up with grey-suited businessmen and rush hour began in the heart of Tokyo.

The next I knew, I was on a completely different train in the middle of the countryside, no-one but old ladies and schoolkids around me as we cut a path through paddy fields and mountains. It was stunningly beautiful. It wasn't Tokyo. It was a problem.

I got off at the next station, a tiny one-track stop serving, I supposed, one or two villages (Japan has a fantastic network of railways that keeps almost everybody within easy reach of at least one line, no matter how rural the area). Cicadas chirped all around me. I tried to check the route finder on my phone but my brain was incapable of deciphering the Japanese characters. I struggled even to check my messages but finally managed to retrieve the dozens that Azumi had sent throughout the night. The general theme was, 'Where the hell are you?' I read the station sign and mailed her my current position – somewhere in Saitama prefecture, I seem to remember – and this brought even more worried texts. I simply felt confused.

I went to the ticket booth and asked them to point me in the right direction for Hirai. 'Is that Hirai... in *Tokyo*?' the man asked, further evidence of just how far off-course I had come. He guided me to the right platform and gave me instructions that included two changes of train company and two hours of travel. I got on the train and, in spite of a couple of extra stops here and there, managed to make it back to my flat eventually. Azumi hadn't gone to work. It took a lot of explaining on my part, a lot of understanding on hers, and the promise of a very expensive dinner before I was able to finally get to bed – thirty hours after I'd woken up for Sports Day.

Oh Shit, I'm Fallin' in Love

I was living in Vancouver, thrilled to be in the most beautiful city on earth but unable to shake off a nagging sense that things weren't right in my life. I had originally come to Canada on a year-long working holiday – fuelled mostly by my lack of any better ideas after finishing university – and quickly fallen in love with the place. This was followed by an enforced return home then a two-year immigration battle until I secured my Permanent Resident status and the right to spend the rest of my life surrounded by the oceans, mountains and forests of British Columbia.

Soon after re-arrival, I secured a part-time job in a clothes shop, a stop-gap until something better came along. Eighteen months later, I was still there. I was sharing an apartment with my sometime writing partner Jake and another friend Lucius in the Italian district of Commercial Drive, enjoying the biscotti and working on unmade film scripts and country songs (*Oh Shit, I'm Fallin' in Love* a particular classic), happy but going nowhere. My twenty-fifth birthday was approaching and my brother Evan was heading to South America on a round-the-world trip. I scraped together the money I'd saved by living off nothing but lettuce sandwiches and flew down to meet him and his then girlfriend in Buenos Aires. A month of bussing around Argentina, Uruguay and Chile sparked an ongoing fascination with Latin America. I wanted more.

In the ferry terminal of Colonia del Sacramento, a gorgeous former Portuguese settlement in southern Uruguay, we contrived to miss the last boat back to Buenos Aires and our hostel. We had somehow misunderstood the announcement to board (a complete lack of Spanish and common sense the major factors) and were happily chatting in the waiting area when we saw the ferry set sail – a cue for much comedy double-taking from us and much laughter from the terminal staff. The only others dim enough to miss it were, embarrassingly, fellow *gringos*, two Americans who lived and worked in Argentina and had popped across the River Plate for the day to update their visas.

The Uruguayan migration officials were closing up for the night but had to re-open their desks to allow us back into the country before showing tremendous patience in taking us to an alternative company's dock nearby and blagging us free passage on the high-speed luxury liner that was just about to depart. As we were hurried through the emigration channel – again – the Chicago boys told us that they were teaching English in Buenos Aires, getting decent pay and enjoying their work. By missing that ferry in Uruguay, the seeds of my future were sown.

Throughout that jet-powered journey (so fast that we actually arrived in Buenos Aires before the ferry we'd missed), throughout our further adventures across Patagonia and the Andes, I concocted the plan: go back to Vancouver, study for an English instructor's qualification, get some teaching practice, study Spanish, then come back to South America for months or years at a time. I eventually achieved almost all of those goals.

After the achingly difficult farewell to my brother, I got back to Canada, reinvigorated and ready to work my guts out to pay for my education. Another year of lettuce sandwiches eventually saved me enough to study for a teaching certificate, but in the meantime I gained experience by volunteering at a Japanese community centre. This was no hardship as most of the students were young graduates who just wanted conversation practice and my visits became a highlight of my week, a break from the day job persuading customers that those khaki pants would look even better with one of our merino wool sweaters. In return for my time I was offered Japanese lessons. As I was already studying Spanish and had no strong intention of going to Asia anytime soon, I wanted to decline but was just too polite to say no. A few weeks later, I was hooked.

The SkyTrain has been a symbol of Vancouver since the World Expo in 1986. It runs along elevated tracks that offer wonderful views of the surrounding peaks and waves, as well as my bedroom – the trains shuddering past just fifteen metres from our apartment – and was my link to downtown, work and my Friday appointment at the Japanese centre. That lunchtime, for the only time among my hundreds of rides on it, the SkyTrain was closed due to a suicide jump. I took the only alternative, a convoluted bus ride after a long wait, and missed both my English and Japanese classes. 'We covered your English hour, and the Japanese teacher went home,' the sympathetic receptionist informed me. 'But if you like there's another available at three. Her name is Azumi.'

The large teaching area looked like a café, tables dotted about the room for small, separate lessons to take place. I sat at number seven in the corner. Right on time, a pretty, sporty-looking girl (I thought she was younger than twenty-seven) bounced over and sat opposite me. She was cheerful and clearly very intelligent, in Canada to study English, work and snowboard. But the first thing I noticed was her cute habit of puckering her lips exaggeratedly whenever she was thinking. She brought a textbook with her, a rarity among the untrained volunteer teachers, suggesting a serious side to her affable character. Best of all, she liked films; not just the latest blockbusters or romantic comedies – although she loved them too – but all kinds of movies from around the world. Within the first few stammered greetings (I was still very much a beginner in the language) I knew that I wanted to see her again. The problem with this was exactly how to go about it. My lack of a love-life in Vancouver had a lot to do with those Canadians' crazy notion of meeting someone, perhaps in a coffee shop, an office, or through a mutual friend, getting their phone number, arranging a date and seeing how things progressed from there. But any success I'd had back in the UK had stemmed from a drunken snog in a disco. While not exactly material for a bestselling romance novel, it was so much easier than having to approach a woman, make it clear that you find her attractive, and risk humiliating rejection in front of anyone within earshot... while stone cold sober. Put simply, I just wasn't very good at it.

For the rest of the hour I tried to think of a good pretence under which to give Azumi my number, finally getting lucky when toward the end of the class she mentioned a film she had seen at the cinema on Commercial Drive. I resorted to English: 'That's near my house. Let me know if ever you're going there again.' I jotted my phone number onto a corner of my notebook, ripped it off and handed it to her. She appeared neither pleased nor displeased. She thanked me politely and left. I went to the bathroom to compose myself.

Once my heart rate slowed down I felt happy that I had taken the risk, any doubts waiting for later when – as is my wont – I would pick apart every sentence of our meeting and convince myself that I'd done everything wrong. I left the building and headed along the pavement towards Granville Street station. Deep in thought, I only noticed very late that I was walking directly behind Azumi. I was worried that I'd say something stupid if we spoke again, and ruin my chances. But if I didn't talk to her and she turned round to see me, she might think I was ignoring her, or – worse – following her. A red light stopped her from crossing Robson Street and I no longer had a choice as I was now standing right next to her.

'Hello. Don't worry, I'm not stalking you.' That was a bad opening. 'I'm just heading home to get ready for a party tonight.' It was a complete lie as the likelihood was that Jake and I would be drinking rye whisky while working on the second verse of *Why Don't I Just Give Up?* But I reckoned that a party might sound less depressing. Azumi smiled.

'I'm meeting some friends later too. You can come if you

88

want, but…'

'Yes. Yes, please. The party isn't a big deal. Actually, there is no party.' I shouldn't have said that. 'I'd love to join you and your friends.'

It took three more weeks of hilarious misunderstandings – I thought she was going out with her classmate Kazu, she thought I was nice but a bit odd (perhaps not a misunderstanding after all) – before we had an actual one-on-one date. Three weeks and a lot more dates later, her visa expired and she had to go home.

What I initially imagined would be a short but sweet romance became a lot more when Azumi returned to Vancouver a few months later. We were a couple. And it was all thanks to that man who, for reasons I never found out, decided his life wasn't worth living and ended it under the wheels of the SkyTrain. I hope he can rest in peace; and I hope that somewhere, somehow, he knows that he didn't die in vain.

Very Countryside

My improving Japanese, my lack of direction in Canada (I later became assistant manager in that stop-gap job, much to my dismay) and, of course, my love for Azumi, all pointed to a fresh start across the Pacific. So, on New Year's Day, Azumi and I said our goodbyes to each other at Vancouver Airport. She boarded the flight to Tokyo and I to Heathrow in order to begin visa procedures and find a job through the London offices of the major Japanese English-teaching agencies.

I soon got an interview with one of the biggest employers of foreign workers in Japan, an agency that sent native English speakers to teach at conversation schools for children and adults throughout the country. My interview went smoothly, they offered me a position and sponsored my visa. They asked where I wished to be posted, I told them Tokyo as my girlfriend lived there, and – a week before I was due to depart – they sent the details of my school. I was stationed in Oyama, a city in Tochigi prefecture. I had heard of neither but was able to find Tochigi on a map, a blob of land where the Kanto plain hits the mountains in the centre of Honshu, the main island in the Japanese archipelago. On my admittedly small map, Oyama was nowhere to be seen, the only thing clear was that it was pretty far from Tokyo. The Japanese Tourist Board in London couldn't help, nor the teaching agency, who were sending me there and refused to be persuaded that I would much prefer a job in one of the hundreds of Tokyo branches.

Azumi discovered that I could reach her local station in just under three hours – not great, but at least we would be able to meet on our days off – although she was also unable to give me any more information on my prospective hometown. I really was flying blind as the JAL 747 took me to Narita airport, accompanied by another new recruit who was in tears because the agency were sending her to a school in central Tokyo after she had insisted on living in the countryside. Neither of us was amused by the irony.

At Narita a company employee met us and put me on a bus to Oyama. 'What's it like?' I enquired.

'I haven't a clue.'

The journey took me past Disneyland, a jarring sight amidst the rice fields of Chiba; past massive nets strung between masts which I first took to be TV signal towers or radar centres but turned out to be golf ranges; past schoolgirls riding bicycles by the side of the river. Despite it being May, the darkness fell early; even in mid-summer it's fully dark by seven, the clocks not adjusting for different seasons. Soon I was unable to make out anything apart from the lights of an occasional village. I was getting deeper into the heart of rural Japan and when the bus stopped to drop off a passenger here and there, all I could hear was the clicking and croaking of cicadas in the trees, frogs in the paddies and crickets in the dry grass.

I knew that Oyama was the final stop and after a few hours

there was only a handful of people left, dozing their way home. Too excited to sleep, I kept my face to the window, interested to see a boy walking home from judo training, still wearing his cream-white *judo gi*, and numerous mini-shrines at the quiet roadsides. I hoped they weren't put there for any reason beyond piety.

We turned a corner and suddenly there was light everywhere. We had hit Oyama and the bus took the long straight route down the main road into the middle of the city, utterly swamped in neon light. Every sign screamed in English, 'Pub', 'Snack Bar' or 'Night Club', and my first thought was that there would be plenty to do in the evenings. I didn't know then that these were all euphemistic terms for hostess bars, where businessmen pay small fortunes to drink and talk with young women, a direct descendant of the geisha culture of the Edo period. Still feeling a little queasy from the shock of all the lights after so much darkness, I met my new colleagues and soon learned that Oyama was a town drawing its strength from a duo of companies – a maker of bulldozers, and the yakuza – and the strip of bars served the workers and clients of both. I resolved to finish the obligatory probation period then request a transfer to Tokyo.

The first couple of weeks, as I completed training and found my bearings in this new city, I counted down each day until I could visit Azumi. That feeling never abated, but I also began to establish myself in Oyama, a place most of my students described as 'very countryside' but – when I factored in the smaller towns touching its borders – had a population the size of Cardiff or downtown Vancouver. Still, the atmosphere was rural, with wide roads, low-slung buildings and rows of dark green hills pushing the city in at the edges, and I started to appreciate Oyama for what it really was: a real, living, breathing town and a place I would have never experienced as a tourist but which allowed me to see the lungs of modern Japan, both agricultural and technological.

A major metropolis, by nature, needs to be international and Tokyo caters admirably to overseas guests; but in doing so it is, ironically, far less Japanese than the rest of the nation. As a child growing up in Leicestershire I always felt that going to London was like visiting another country: tourists and businesspeople from all over the world, entertainments and amenities geared towards these visitors, its British-ness almost a parody of itself with union flags dangling off every building and lamp post. Fantastic as London is, to get a taste of the real UK I always recommend my foreign friends go… anywhere else. The same can be said of Paris, Beijing or Rome, practically separate entities within the countries they govern.

By staying in Tochigi I would have to adapt to the local life and study the language with real vigour, unlike a lot of Tokyo-based friends who spent their free time in overpriced but foreigner-friendly *gaijin* bars, getting by with English and a phrasebook. I chose to stay in Oyama even after my probation ended. It was a selfish decision not to transfer but I believe it kept my relationship with Azumi fresh and exciting, our days together special and our days apart filled with anticipation.

I stayed in Oyama for two and a half years, making good friends, joining a rugby team and drinking unbelievably cheap drinks at about the only normal bar on that glowing central strip affectionately known as *Sukebe dori* – Pervert Street. In fact, this nickname was used so often that a couple of new teachers, unaware of the translation, thought it was its real name; I can only imagine the look on locals' faces when these foreign women asked them, 'Can you tell me how to get to Pervert Street, please?' In contrast to its seedy neighbours, the bar was a traditional *izakaya* with an easy-going atmosphere, chatty staff and friendly clientele. I felt very much the local there, all the more so when I started making use of their 'bottle keep' service. This, I later realised, was quite common throughout Japan: if customers don't finish all two litres of their *shochu* or *sake* (which, incidentally, is actually called *Nihonshu* – 'Japanese liquor' – in its homeland; *sake* is a generic term for any alcoholic drink), then they can write their name on the bottle and store it on a shelf until a later date. The staff would often add messages or cartoons of their own, adding a frisson of expectation to the next visit.

Everything was going perfectly in my new home, until I got promoted at work.

Laundry Detergent for Half-Wits

While it's very flattering to be asked, I've never quite understood how being good at a job suddenly qualifies you to take on a position of management. Thanks to positive comments from students and colleagues, I was aware that I was a pretty decent teacher and, in the fast-turnover world of conversation schools, it wasn't long before I was one of the more experienced members of the team, so I knew that I was a logical choice when one of the senior trainers left Japan. I also knew that I would be useless as a boss. I loved teaching but just wasn't interested in making schedules and organising meetings. In confrontations I have a terrible habit of going red and shaking, so I hated dealing with some of the less enthusiastic teachers who worked there. The school was very good at taking care of employees when they first came to Japan, always available for advice about any aspect of living in a new country. Sadly, this caused a significant minority to become utterly dependent on the company and indignant when things were not a hundred percent perfect. My favourite complaint was, 'Garett, the curtains in my apartment are dirty. What are you going to do about it?' I felt like I was spending more time dealing with petty gripes and administration (and buying laundry detergent for half-wits) than I was with students. It was time for a change. It was time to grow up. It was time to take the plunge, move to Tokyo and get a flat with Azumi.

After inspecting, in the words of the estate agent, 'More apartments than any other customer this year,' we settled on the first place we'd looked at – a modern one-bedroom place near Hirai station – and I found a job at another conversation school on the west side of Tokyo.

Azumi and I were living together. Inevitably there were teething troubles but, on the whole, it felt right, and it was brilliant to see her every morning and every evening. And it was good, too, to be able to relax on our days off instead of always taking long train rides just to meet each other. As fun as it had been to rendezvous once a week, it also put a lot of pressure on us to *do something* – see a film, go to a museum, have a fancy meal. Living together, we could still do all of those whenever we wanted but we could also just take it easy around the flat if we felt like it, stroll to the nearby river, or kick a ball about in the park, and I found out that Azumi had a heck of a right foot on her.

Patience was one of Azumi's best qualities and she adapted to my morning grumpiness with remarkable ease, while I soon got used to the stench of her breakfast *natto*, even if I still thought it smelled like sweaty feet. And that patience kept her on my side even when I probably didn't deserve it, even when I stayed for two and a half years in Tochigi, even when I dragged her along to watch rugby matches at a sports bar in the middle of the night, and even when I stayed out till the early hours in Shibuya. But, far from being the submissive servant woman of Japanese stereotype, she was a scrappy, adventurous person, more than happy to backpack around Europe on her own, or eat at the dingiest restaurants in Bolivia and Thailand.

Back in Canada, long before I met Azumi, I had watched a seminar at the Vancouver Film Festival featuring the Farrelly brothers. Discussing their 1998 movie, *There's Something About Mary*, they explained their thought process when creating the title character. They said that whenever a friend had been on a date their first question to him was always, 'Does she have a sense of humour?' If the friend answered yes then the second question was, 'Just a laugh-at-your-jokes sense of humour? Or a bust-your-balls sense of humour?' As far as they were concerned, the latter was the perfect kind of woman. Mary had a bust-your-balls sense of humour. So did Azumi. This made her great at meeting my friends too. I never had to worry about her being able to make conversation, because she was a lot better at it than me, happily chatting away within seconds of meeting someone new – male or female – and capable of giving as good as she got when the jokes started flying. At these times, at a party or *izakaya* when she was deep in discussion or trading barbs with a friend, I could take a step back and become a spectator for a moment, and I could really see what an amazing person Azumi was. Basically, she was a good'un, and I was a very lucky man.

Just Like Vegas

When I started drinking beer as a teenager, hangovers were an abstract notion, something I was vaguely aware of but couldn't really pin down. Before long they became physical entities, the morning after a heavy night spent within easy distance of a toilet and a carton of paracetamol. In my late twenties these mornings stretched on until teatime, and now hangovers had become lingering conditions, expanding for two or three days like self-inflicted flu. On Tuesday morning I was still feeling sticky and tired, a sensation not dissimilar to jet lag, as I rode the train to work.

I was joined by Graeme, the ALT at the neighbouring school who had filled me with dread during the area meeting at the beginning of term. His overly dramatic warning to be careful at my school was, as I'd suspected, referring to Ms Hasebe. He had worked with her for a week the previous year so had first-hand knowledge of her foibles. He also gave me a juicy piece of gossip that explained so much about her obsession with my predecessor – she and Pete had been a couple. As far as I knew they were both single at the time so good luck to them, but it made it impossible for me to live up to her image of Pete; it also made it impossible for me to respect a man who had sunk that low, so from that point on whenever Hasebe said, 'Pete used to…' I could take it with a large pinch of salt. There were many things Pete used to do that I would not be emulating.

By coincidence, Graeme lived at the next station from mine and his school was served by the same Metro stop, so we would frequently bump into one another on our journey to and from work. It was good to have someone in a similar position to share stories and offload frustrations, but Graeme had an annoying trait of thinking he knew the answer to everything. If I said, 'God, my third years just wouldn't shut up today,' he would force upon me glaringly obvious tidbits of advice such as, 'You should try to give them activities that will keep them interested.' When I complained about Ms Hasebe he was certain that his five days working with her made him more qualified than me on knowing how to handle her craziness. In the end I had to keep my comments as neutral as possible so as not to get more irritated by his condescension.

Graeme and I had a lot in common. Both British, we shared the same current job and we had both worked for a few years at conversation schools before becoming ALTs. This meant that we had been in Japan for longer than the average teacher. Like me, Graeme had a solid command of the language, lived with his Japanese girlfriend and planned on sticking around for the foreseeable future. But unlike me, he appeared to hate the place. On top of that, he didn't like his own country much either. He also had an almost pathological obsession with the stupidity of Americans, the crassness of Australians and the cold efficiency of Germans. For some reason he didn't mind the French. And because he was so sure that he knew everything, he would voice his opinions as non-debatable facts: 'Americans are children. Dangerous, stupid children with too much power.'

'Well, I'm sure they're not all–'

'Dangerous children.'

'Umm, OK then.'

He insisted that everyone in the UK was unfriendly and dour, without exception, but then complained about the racism of the Japanese if a local person dared say anything disparaging about British food or weather. His assertions that he didn't have many real friends at home and didn't want any hinted at a man who was in Japan to get away from something, a sadly common factor in a lot of people coming here. For some reason, many misfits and loners believe that Japanese people won't notice their weirdness, or mistake it for charming eccentricity. Sadly for them, Japanese people aren't stupid.

After a couple of months, I had become accustomed to the rush hour train ride but whenever I shared it with Graeme he would snarl and sneer at all the fellow passengers, shocked that on public transport he might come into contact with other human beings. He tutted loudly every time more commuters boarded, his favourite line being a sarcastic 'Room for one more,' usually while glaring at whoever was standing next to him. It never crossed his mind for a moment that he too was one of the passengers taking up space in the carriage; or that his constant shoving and shouting was disturbing others far more than they were disturbing him. As far as he was concerned, Tokyo was a city founded, developed and populated merely to get on his nerves, and it was his right to let 'Them' (he constantly used the third person plural as a thinly-veiled substitute for 'Those nasty Japanese') know about it in no uncertain terms. All I could do was smile apologetically and sigh with relief when we reached our station, not least because – to top it all – Graeme had extraordinarily bad breath.

It was strange to prepare for Sports Day again. Being a weekday, there were even fewer spectators, but the sun was shining brightly, the sharp light piercing through my fragile skull. I was curious to see how Messrs Kubo and Shimada would be acting after their battle on Sunday night. Would they be contrite? Would they be aggressive? Would they be embarrassed? In actuality they were none of those, just carrying on as if nothing had happened, much in the same way as friendliness at a party wasn't usually transferred to the staffroom on a Monday morning. In this case it was a relief not to have to grab onto any jacket tails to prevent a brawl, but I still found it odd that such strong emotions could be so easily pushed aside. When I asked Ms Maki if they had been OK when they'd arrived at work – my starting time being later than theirs – she seemed bemused that I would ask such a thing. 'Of course they were OK. Why?' Just like Vegas, what happens at the office party, clearly stays at the office party.

Superman and Keystone Cops

The blue tarpaulin was pulled off the damp wooden chairs at last, and the remaining sports events could be held. The third years had a rather exciting race around the track ending in a mass tug-of-war involving sixty participants. Like all of the other games, it was accompanied by music over the loudspeakers, and the *Superman* march at full blast added to the adrenalin rush. Mr Kubo was the MC and obviously had a wonderful time selecting the soundtrack for Sports Day. *Chariots of Fire* was an obvious but exhilarating choice for the straight relays, *The Big Country* for the *Rawhide* lasso game, and *Tubular Bells* for the gymnastics display. The undercurrent of sexism was heightened by the comedy *Keystone Cops*-style tunes whenever the girls had to do any running, in contrast to the heroism of John Williams and Vangelis for the boys.

The *Looney Tunes* theme would have been much more fitting for the boys' relay race. Despite the batons being painted to match the colours of the respective teams, Taro kun managed to get confused on the first handover and pass his yellow baton to Kouki, in the red team. Kouki took the baton perfectly, eyes forward as he broke into a sprint. His double take was priceless when he realised he'd been given the wrong one, and he looked back to see what he should do. Masa, in the yellows, had been waiting for Taro's baton but was now empty-handed, and Noriyuki, holding the red baton, had no-one to give it to because his teammate Kouki had already run off with the yellow one. He shrugged and gave it to Masa, and the race continued. Only the blues, lagging well behind, didn't get mixed up in the debacle. The race was epic, with every male in every class in the school taking a two-hundred-metre leg, and went on for another five minutes or so, the yellows finally edging out the reds in a dramatic photo finish. The blues, a team filled with dossers and geeks, trailed well behind having been lapped by both of their rivals. The sarcastic applause as they finished soon turned to laughter when it was announced that the red and yellow teams were both disqualified for the illegal handover; the blues were the winners.

This story would be nothing more than a mildly amusing anecdote if it weren't for the attitude of the kids towards Sports Day. It may have only been an intra-school event with just three possible champions, but it took on huge emotional significance for most of the students, teenage boys and girls weeping unashamedly based on their individual and team performances, the blood they shed throughout the practices a symbol of their almighty efforts. Poor Taro was inconsolable after his error had cost his side so dearly. Luckily for him, the yellows finally sealed overall victory and the roar of triumph echoed off the surrounding skyscrapers causing windows to open in curiosity. The reds and blues were crestfallen, t-shirts thrown to the ground in disgust, tears smearing the dust that coated their faces. I was to see this intensity of feeling at other times during the year and I wondered if it was healthy to build up so much pressure. Before Sports Day, athletics meetings, concerts, school plays and – most seriously of all – exams, all the practice, all the rehearsals, all the effort, got concentrated into one or two weeks when everything else was pushed aside as unimportant. Perhaps there were benefits in the students focusing on one thing at a time in order to do the best they possibly could, but I was worried that, by making Sports Day or any other single event so all-consuming, then the price of failure became agonisingly high.

I've mentioned previously the surprising Japanese propensity for tears. There's an almost fetishistic fascination with pain and suffering, never better captured than in these kinds of sporting events. The national high school baseball championship is held every spring and summer in Osaka. Koshien stadium is the home of Hanshin Tigers, one of the most popular professional clubs in the country, but twice a year it hosts the top school teams from across Japan in a tournament screened live on the major TV networks. Personally, I think the idol-worship of schoolkids is a bit odd, but the ratings are high and the star players soon become household names. Now, if you watch a Tigers game at Koshien, their uniforms are always spotlessly clean, the well-tended ground yielding no more than the occasional grass stain. But in preparation for the high school competition, extra mud is actually *shipped in* and strategically placed at the bases. The teenage players, all wearing white, soon become caked in dirt, producing perfect photo opportunities for the national press and evening news. The encapsulation of effort and passion is ensured through a few blobs of mud. And the images chosen by the media are very rarely shots of the boys in pitching and slugging

104

action; they are of the defeated team bawling with grief at a young dream shattered, the camera zooming in invasively. On TV this will usually be accompanied by some melancholic piano music, to really hammer home the youth's agony, and a cut-back to the studio just in time to see the newsreader stoically wipe a tear from his cheek before somehow managing to continue with the broadcast.

As a fanatical sports player and watcher, I know that there's nothing more annoying than people saying, 'It's only a game,' particularly when I'm in the midst of feeling sorry for myself about my team's latest capitulation. But I also can't see any point in accentuating the negatives and wallowing in defeat, especially when the sport in question is a piggy back race while wearing multi-coloured comedy wigs. But the intensity of the Sports Day build-up made tears inevitable, and two-thirds of the students went home in despair.

Tokyo Land

It felt strange going to the airport without a rucksack or suitcase. The seventy-minute train ride to Narita Airport was surprisingly pleasant. Tokyo's main international gateway is actually located forty miles away in Chiba prefecture, the line cutting through a corridor of forests, villages and temples, and I was happy to leave my book closed and enjoy the view as I anticipated the days ahead. My brother Evan and his wife Wendy were coming to stay.

Knowing that they would have taken an overnight flight – going east is always a killer – my slight headache after a late night and early rise felt right, an act of solidarity leaving us all in similar condition. My slightly dishevelled appearance, however, didn't impress the security guards as I walked from the underground station to the airport proper. After numerous searches and questions I was allowed to enter the arrivals hall, in perfect time to see Evan and Wendy walk through the gate.

These moments had become a lot easier now that my brothers were married. We were never the most demonstrative family and no matter how much I would have liked to, it never felt appropriate to hug the male members of my the clan. But now, instead of awkward pats on the arm and muttered hellos hiding our elation, I could let all the pent-up emotion flow into my hugs for their wives. Then, before we knew it, we were talking about the films they watched on the plane, the latest football news and our plans for the day (sleep being the number one priority), and it was as if we'd never been apart.

After reaching the apartment and reuniting with Azumi (they had all met many times before, most recently at Evan and Wendy's wedding the previous summer), we took that promised nap, then headed out to see the sights of Hirai.

Evan and Wendy's previous visit had been when I lived in Tochigi, and our time in Tokyo spent in the usual tourist areas of Shibuya and Ginza, so this was their first taste of *shitamachi* – downtown Tokyo, the place where local people live and die and buy their groceries. After a year in Hirai I had come to consider it fairly tame compared to most districts – packed full of shops, restaurants and aging blocks of flats but somewhere that even the most dyed-in-the-wool Tokyoites struggled to place on a map. Evan and Wendy, though, loved it, coining a phrase I've seen fit to use many times since: 'Tokyo Land'. The buildings, especially in front of the station, were so close together and so covered in neon that they looked like a small-scale parody of Japan's capital, as if they were merely façades in a theme park or movie set. Electronic music rang out from stores, traffic lights and station announcements; schoolkids weaved past on bicycles, chattering loudly in (I'd almost forgotten) the most foreign of languages. The *kanji* signs were completely indecipherable; even the ubiquitous golden arches of McDonald's were accompanied by the swishing strokes of the *katakana* alphabet. Ironically, the buildings most likely to use English were the most Japanese of entertainments – karaoke, *pachinko* game centres and love hotels.

Suddenly, I was seeing everything through new eyes and I realised how amazing it all was. It was actually quite disconcerting, and I felt like a tightrope walker, strolling happily along the wire until someone suggested I look down. For Evan and Wendy it was all so unfamiliar, spectacular and surprising that I was forced once again to think, *How the hell did I end up here?*

Before I was completely overcome by vertigo we stopped at a café for lip-smatteringly bitter coffee. Evan commented on the tininess of the cartons of cream provided with the blacker than black drinks. They are about half the size of those in other countries, giving Evan a brief taste of life as a giant, as his fingers struggled clumsily to snap the miniscule seal. Wendy coughed theatrically, reminding me that customers were smoking on the adjacent table. Japan is still very much in thrall to the tobacco companies, and it's now one of the few developed nations without a smoking ban in restaurants. To a European, it seemed almost prehistoric for someone to light up in such a confined space, and again I was reminded that things had changed in the time I'd been away from home. Britain had changed, my family had changed... and, I supposed, I had changed too. Any sense of unease was soon dispelled as we chatted for hours through the haze of smoke. Whenever any friends or family came to visit Japan, we were duty bound to do some sightseeing and tick the 'Been there, done that' boxes. These were always fascinating – you don't get too many Shinto shrines or fifty-foot statues of Buddha where I come from – but the moments that always stuck with me were these times spent in bars and coffee shops, talking in an easy way that was impossible through our frequent phone calls and e-mails. Living abroad entailed many sacrifices, the most obvious being the distance from loved ones, but I also felt lucky to be able to really appreciate our brief moments together when a year's build-up of random conversation could be released in a few memorable days.

There were practical things to consider too, as we planned the following week's excursion to Kyoto for an old school friend's wedding. Azumi had once again come up trumps, finding a cheap package deal for the hotel and *shinkansen* ('bullet train', the more recognisable term among foreigners, is utterly unknown and unused in Japan). Now we just had to decide when to go and what to do when we weren't toasting the bride and groom.

But for the most part we just relaxed and nattered, the strong coffee injecting some energy into our bodies, enabling us to set out again and stroll through the local shopping arcade.

The rather ramshackle mall had recently suffered extensive damage from a massive fire that blazed for a day and a night but, in true Japanese style, the melted walls and roof had been completely renovated in about the same length of time. This always confounded me, the way buildings and roads were constantly being erected, gutted, then erected again, a never-ending cycle of construction that led to any apartment block more than ten years old being considered old and decrepit – a boon when looking for a bargain home. It also kept the unemployment rate at virtually zero, and builders were a common sight on the trains and streets, their distinctive outfits of outrageously baggy trousers (somewhere in the MC Hammer range) and *geta* shoes (basically just split-toe socks on a rubber sole) an easily identifiable throwback to feudal times when each occupation was expected to don specific uniforms, and no doubt the cause of countless deaths and severed digits. I gave up trying to comprehend the arbitrary swings between the desire for the new (pre-owned cars and houses considered by most Japanese to be dirty and unusable) and, on the other hand, the desperate cling to tradition – the dangers of flapping clothes and cotton footwear on a construction site littered with chainsaws, steel girders and fifty-foot drops not seemingly apparent. Still, a few fatalities were always good for the funeral business.

We browsed through a secondhand clothes shop (used apparel is OK, for some reason), Evan picking up a natty retro T-shirt indicating that he was a member of the high school ping pong club, then headed for another of my favourite Japanese institutions – the hundred yen shop. Back home I'd seen pound shops, and Canada had its dollar stores, but these names were used loosely, the reality of inflation and market forces meaning we could rarely find anything that really was so cheap. But these hundred yen (equivalent to about seventy pence or one US dollar) places really were *one hundred yen* places – give or take eight percent tax. Plates, mugs and dishes for a hundred each, kids' toys for a hundred, gardening equipment for – you guessed it – a hundred; CDs, computer software, stationery, electric extension cords (a risky one, that), bathroom supplies, ornaments, magazines, books, snacks, drinks, light bulbs… I'm not sure how they managed it, and my conscience probably didn't want to know, but they were the greatest shops on earth, a huge contradiction to the myth of Japan as an expensive place to live. The only downside was that it was so easy to drop a few thousand yen on a basketful of stuff, the temptation to add just one more thing too strong to resist – it's only a hundred yen, after all! We left with a few bags of kitchen utensils, an extra towel for the guests, a couple of dumbbells that I would use at least twice, and a therapeutic eye mask that is probably still in its packaging. We went home and had another nap.

Undead Horse Mackerel

Feeling slightly refreshed after our siesta, we headed out that evening for my favourite bar, a local *izakaya* called *Guridochin*, specialising in *yakitori* – chicken on a stick – in various forms: breast, wing, skin, cartilage, liver, tongue; in sauce or with salt; plain or minced; accompanied with vegetables or by themselves. Before coming to Japan I had never realised that such a small creature could be so versatile, the Japanese experts at making use of every part of a dead animal. Not only was the chicken (served on a refillable bed of raw cabbage, just to vary the diet a little) delicious, it was also very reasonable and at fifty yen a stick the problem was similar to that experienced in the hundred yen shop – when to stop.

I had mulled over the bar's name for months – *Guridochin* bore no resemblance to any Japanese words I knew – until Azumi explained that it was a shortened version of 'grilled chicken', borrowed from English and mutated in the way only Japanese-English knows how. In a similar vein, the personal computer is called a *paso kon*, convenience stores *konbini* and police patrol cars *pato ka*.

It's not uncommon for the head of froth on a beer to be bigger than the drink itself in *izakaya*; it's said to keep the flavour locked in but I can't help feeling that was just a myth created by the breweries – we'd barely taken a few sips before it was time to order another round. These came along with endless supplies of skewered chicken, and we talked until the early hours, enjoying the traditional but very down-to-earth atmosphere. The restaurant space was not much larger than an average living room, making for an intimate ambience where fellow customers' conversations could be heard almost as clearly as our own. The walls were made of bamboo, the high shelves covered in ancient-looking bottles of *sake*, and the tiny kitchen area was fully visible behind the narrow counter. In the corner was a large fish tank in which a school of *aji* swam around happily. (I later learned that this particular fish is called horse mackerel in English. Due to the stunning variety of seafood eaten here – often up to fifty kinds on a single menu – my knowledge of fish species is now far more extensive in Japanese than in my own language.)

When we were all suitably merry, Azumi and I decided to play our usual lame joke by ordering some sashimi then watching our guests' faces as the *aji* was fished out of the tank, a few minutes later emerging at our table, sliced perfectly, speared through with a kebab stick but still flapping and moving its eyes and mouth in a slightly flummoxed fashion. It was, of course, already dead, but the muscles and nerve endings hadn't caught up to this fact yet, causing the prolonged twitching. This one was particularly tenacious, moving for a good fifteen minutes as we tucked into its soft and very tasty meat – once our guests' initial shock had subsided.

Finally, too full for any more beer, chicken or undead fish, we shared a bottle of *awamori*, a distilled rice liquor from Okinawa, lethally strong and dangerously easy to drink. I had first tasted it on a

113

trip to its home island where locals would always offer me a glass despite being a total stranger, and every sip since has been laced with memories of that wonderful holiday – palm tree beaches, pure white coral reef and the friendliest people of anywhere in Japan. It was a perfect way to end the day and, jetlagged or not, we all slept soundly.

On the Sunday we headed for a more touristy venue, taking the Sobu line further than my usual stop, then switching to the circular Yamanote line, a vein linking the most pulsating places in the city. On the edge of Yoyogi Park, a huge streak of green right in the centre of Tokyo, we reached a rather quaint little station, one side shaded by trees, the other fronted by a wall resembling a Tudor house. The façade couldn't have been more deceptive; this was Harajuku, the funkiest, trendiest and weirdest district in Japan.

Exiting on the opposite side to the park, we could instantly see Takeshita dori, a narrow pedestrian street teeming with teenagers and, well, people like us, just wanting to gawp at this amazing sight. A large percentage of people were dressed in the *Loli gosu* style. In another corruption from English, this actually means 'Lolita gothic' and perfectly sums up the look: Little Bo Peep dresses, lined with outrageous frills and lace, punk hair and striking make-up. And it wasn't limited to the females.

When I had first come here, I remember thinking, *Where do they buy these costumes?* The answer presented itself within seconds, as Takeshita dori was home to dozens of shops specialising in wild fashions, fetish goods and – don't ask me why – crepes. The effect was dizzying, pink and black all around, and music and voices blaring loudly. On the street itself it was almost impossible to stop and take it all in; we just had to keep moving with the crowds, feeling very much the innocents abroad as our eyes bulged and chins dropped. Wendy asked the very sensible question, 'Where are they all going, dressed up like that?' In fact most of them had no destination in particular. They were simply dressing up for the fun of it, which is probably the best reason of all. Really, it was rather wonderful how these young men and women could cross-dress and fancy-dress to their heart's content, without fear of being ridiculed, taunted, or rounded on by thugs with cricket bats. I'm sure Japan has gained its high status in the fashion world in no small part because – outside the conservative company culture – people can wear whatever they like and no-one else appears to give a damn.

As we headed back in the direction of Yoyogi Park, we came across a group of men practicing rockabilly dance steps, their leather jackets and quiffs adding authenticity to the moves. This would have been a mild distraction compared to some of the more way-out costumes, but these men were probably old enough to have actually *been* rockabillies during the 1950s. Their beer bellies jiggled with every twist, and no amount of hair cream could hide the grey, but they moved with a precision and smoothness that betrayed years of rehearsals and performances, and it was oddly moving. Any visitor wanting to stereotype the Japanese middle-aged male as a robotic worker-drone would have been utterly flummoxed by the sight.

Deeper into the park and the fashions became more subdued, along with the thick, dark green of the trees. While the park lay between some of the most hectic districts in the city, the noise of traffic and weekend bustle seemed to be absorbed and cushioned by the leaves and branches. The air became noticeably cooler as we stepped under the massive *torii* gate – the biggest of its kind in the country. A rare Tokyo silence fell upon us as we entered Meiji Shrine, the capital's major centre for Shintoism.

There's a wonderful pragmatism about religion in Japan, friends of mine happily praying at Buddhist temples, Shinto shrines and – at weddings, at least – Christian churches, without any sense of hypocrisy or insincerity. So I felt no embarrassment at throwing a few coins into the tray, breathing in the thick incense smoke and putting my hands together. A marriage ceremony taking place in the huge wooden complex reminded me of our friend's imminent nuptials, so I muttered my best wishes in the prayer.

The shaven-headed monks and nuns milling around the shrine in pure white gowns lent an austerity to the scene, although my image of priests as paragons of virtue had been tarnished somewhat by a couple of students I had taught at my old conversation school. Before my first class with each of them I had felt very nervous, unsure whether topics such as alcohol, romantic relationships, even meat-eating, would be taboo. As it turned out, both – one a Shinto priest and one Buddhist – were heavy drinking, carnivorous womanisers. The only nod to spirituality came when the Shinto follower told me that he liked to climb the highest mountains in the

116

Andes and the Rockies without oxygen, food or human accompaniment. 'It clears my mind,' he explained.

The Buddhist, after the textbook mentioned Christmas, casually asked if I was Christian. Rather humbly, I had to confess to my dithering agnosticism.

'I think there's probably *something* else, but I'm not sure if any one religion can really give me all the answers.'

He nodded sagely and thought for a few seconds. 'Very Zen.' It pleased me greatly.

She Loves You

As I strolled along the carriage, it occurred to me that at that moment I may just have been the fastest man on earth. The fields on either side of the bullet train were mere smudges of green as we hurtled south-west of Tokyo at three hundred kilometres an hour. Add the five miles an hour or so that I was walking, and I doubt that anyone in the world was moving any quicker than me as I headed to the toilet towards the front of the train.

Shinkansen literally means 'new trunk line', a name not nearly as sexy as the one by which it's known throughout the English-speaking world – the Bullet Train. The first version was completed just in time for the opening of the 1964 Tokyo Olympics, linking the capital to the second largest metropolis, Osaka, five hundred kilometres away. That journey now takes less than two and a half hours as it cuts through the suburbs, fields and mountains down the southern flank of the country.

The last stop before reaching Shin-Osaka station is Kyoto – the old capital of Japan – and this was our planned destination. Azumi, Evan, Wendy and I tucked into *eki-ben*, 'train station lunchboxes' filled with steak, rice and salad, hurtled past that great Japanese icon, Mt Fuji, its perfect cone still covered in snow even in July, and discussed our plan for the next few days. Our old school friend, Allan, had lived in Kyoto for the past two years, working for an IT company. Soon after arriving, he met Ryoko in a local bar, fell in love, and – I had shifted uncomfortably when I relayed the news to Azumi – proposed within a few months. After a prolonged engagement, they were finally getting married this weekend.

We arrived in central Kyoto, the station a startlingly modernist building – all glass and steel – which seemed at odds with the city's reputation as the centre for traditional culture. Our hotel was just a few minutes' walk away, an uninspiring block-shaped edifice but clean and comfortable inside. We dropped our bags off and decided to do some sightseeing before meeting Allan and Ryoko that evening.

Nijo Castle was a wooden fortification built by the great Tokugawa shogunate in the seventeenth century. It served as the centre of the imperial court in the west, even as the capital city moved east to Edo (now Tokyo), and must have been an impressive sight for visitors at the time. Huge ornate wall paintings decorated the rooms and gold leaf covered much of the ceilings. The paper doors and wide spaces made it surprisingly open, and one could imagine catching glimpses of the shogun and his family through cracks between the sliding doors. The inhabitants were heavily protected, of course, with hidden chambers built in to conceal bodyguards who could appear from the wall to surprise would-be assassins. And, in case of ninja attack at night, the floorboards of the corridor were designed to squeak whenever someone stepped on them, earning them the nickname *uguisubari* – nightingale floors.

Upon leaving the castle, we wanted to get a snack; and here

we ran into one of the problems with this city. Speak to any Japanese person and the image you will get of Kyoto is of a town steeped in history and culture, like emerging from a time tunnel to walk the streets of the old capital and imagine samurai and geisha milling around you. The reality is rather disappointing. There are undoubtedly a lot of interesting temples, shrines and castles, and one or two small areas that still retain a flavour of ancient Japan. But city planning rules are very lax throughout the country, so UNESCO-registered World Heritage Sites will be flanked by 1980s apartments towers or faceless brick buildings, and there seemed to be no efforts to accommodate visitors around the major sites. We circled Nijo Castle, desperately searching for a café, or even a shop that might sell drinks. All we could find were eerily quiet office blocks.

This was actually my fourth trip to the city, it being a requisite destination for anyone who came to visit me, and – to be absolutely honest – I was getting sick of the place. I always seemed to spend more time traipsing between sites than actually enjoying them, and all the cafes and restaurants seemed to be concentrated in small areas, not always near any of the major destinations. It felt very familiar to be stumbling around generic city blocks in search of a coffee shop, all of us becoming increasingly grumpy, until we finally found an otherwise empty café on an anonymous side street.

With some food and drink inside us, we felt energised enough to catch a taxi and set out for Kinkakuji, the Golden Temple, so called because its exterior is entirely covered in gold leaf. We took photos in front of the temple, its reflection sparkling in the adjacent pond as the evening sun bathed us in a tangerine glow, and we began to feel more positive about the place.

By the time darkness fell, we had arrived in Gion, the old entertainment district, famous for its geisha girls and drinking holes. This is one of the few areas of Kyoto to maintain a real sense of the past, and we were all thrilled to catch a glimpse of a couple of geisha walking down a narrow lamplit alleyway (although there is a good chance they were simply tourists who had paid to dress up in the traditional kimono and pure white make-up, but I'll presume the more romantic possibility). Here in Gion, we were reunited with Allan and his fiancée Ryoko, and they took us to an *okonomiyaki* restaurant nearby. Actually a dish from neighbouring Osaka, *okonomiyaki* means 'fry what you like' and is a savoury pancake in which we can add seafood, pork, vegetables... as the name says, pretty much anything we want. We cooked the dish ourselves, on a hot plate in the centre of our table, and it occurred to me that food in Japan is so often about the experience as much as the taste. It was great to catch up with old friends as we took turns in mixing the ingredients and pouring the batter, then flipping the pancakes over and adding the rich dark sauce, mayonnaise and dried bonito flakes that curled and wriggled as they touched the hot food – reminding Wendy of the half-dead horse mackerel we'd eaten a few days earlier.

The wedding was the next day, but Allan and Ryoko surprised us by revealing that they had actually become husband and wife that afternoon. In Japan, weddings are purely for show, with the legal signing of marriage certificates only allowed at city hall, usually a drab grey administration building on the edge of town. Allan told me that it was actually quite disconcerting just how easy it was. They could walk up to the desk without an appointment, show their ID, sign a few pieces of paper, and within minutes they were Mr and Mrs. In fact, most city halls, while officially closed at night, have a security guard on duty who is authorised to give and receive the necessary marriage documents, meaning that Japan is like one big Las Vegas, quickie weddings available twenty-four hours a day.

The next morning we had time to take in my favourite Kyoto site, Sanjusangendo, a long wooden hall shaped like the stand of a sports stadium. But instead of football supporters, the terracing held over a thousand Buddhist *kannon*, life-size cypress statues, each figure completely different from its neighbour. These statues are between seven hundred and nine hundred years old and were a humbling site as we shuffled in front of them all, bewitched by their lifeless stares.

Our bus back to the hotel got caught in a traffic jam – another feature of Kyoto, the weekend seeing it clogged up with tourists' cars – so we rushed to change into our wedding gear then ran to the local shrine for the ceremony. The insidious humidity of summer was just beginning, so Azumi, Evan, Wendy and I must have looked like drowned ducks as we sweated and panted our way into the courtyard. After an overcast morning, the sun was shining now so we found a shaded spot just to the side of the main shrine, and here we bumped into Allan – fully dressed in the black kimono of the groom, his curly light-brown hair incongruous in these most Japanese of circumstances. He was probably the only one present who was sweating more than us, having spent the last thirty minutes being pushed and pulled into the traditional ceremonial robes. But I have to admit, he looked pretty good, like Tom Cruise in *The Last Samurai*.

Then the bridal party arrived and we caught sight of Ryoko. In stark contrast to Allan's dark attire, her kimono was white as snow, with shimmering red lining. Her make-up, too, was white, not dissimilar to the geisha we had spotted in Gion, and an elaborate headdress and wig covered her hair.

The bride, groom and guests entered the small shrine, listened to the Shinto priest's incantations then sipped the saucers of *sake* that were handed to us. It was a short ceremony but moving and memorable, the humming chants of the priest and monks ringing through our ears for the rest of the day.

The entire party exited the shrine together then posed for photographs. Our perspiration had thankfully dried by now, and the glorious sunshine meant that Ryoko's white kimono positively glowed, so it was a beautiful sight – the happy couple flanked by family and close friends in a mix of Western-style suits and dresses, and Eastern robes.

Another feature of Japanese weddings is the number of changes of clothing the bride and groom are expected to make. We were ushered to a nearby hotel where we could sip on drinks, before Allan and Ryoko appeared before us again – this time in decidedly un-Japanese tuxedo and wedding dress. There would be two more changes later – formal party wear, then more casual evening clothes – and Azumi told us that this was quite conservative compared to many weddings, where the bride would change dresses with almost every dinner course.

There were tearful speeches (the Japanese love of a good cry on show for all to see), countless small dishes, free-flowing beer and *sake*, and – to my surprise – comedy skits. Friends of the bride sang songs and donned rainbow-coloured wigs in routines that had clearly required a certain amount of practice, and some of Allan's local friends did a short comedy routine that consisted mostly of slapping each other on the head. This is quite common at wedding parties, and with all of the speeches too – from family, friends, bosses, colleagues – it made for a long dinner. Evan, Wendy and I felt that we should smile and nod appreciatively during every performance – even though most of it was of course in Japanese – but as I looked around I noticed that very few other people were paying any attention. This was something I had seen in many official functions I'd attended with work too. Give a Japanese person a microphone and you'll struggle to get it off them again – but nobody will listen. It was almost as if there was a tacit agreement that we must all perform the rituals and mark the moment by soliloquising and serenading the happy couple; but there was no need for anyone to actually take on board what was being said. While one poor group of Ryoko's old classmates was singing an acapella version of the Beatles' *She Loves You*, the intended audience was tucking into dessert, chatting to their friends or – in the case of nearly every man over the age of fifty – openly sleeping.

You Need Them More Than Me

The more formal banquet finally over, it was time for the less formal after-party. Our hotel was just around the corner, so we could rush to our rooms, do a quick change into clothes more suited to thirty-degree heat, and set out for the small standing-room-only bar for the night. Much like weddings anywhere in the world, we'd had comparatively little chance to actually talk to the bride and groom on their big day, so it was good to catch up with Allan and Ryoko, as well as Allan's parents and brother who had flown out for the occasion.

The atmosphere was decidedly wilder than the earlier Shinto shrine and sit-down meal, and it only got more raucous as the night progressed and the party moved to a dingy pool room (for reasons unknown to me). The international flavour led to a number of cross-continental hook-ups, a fair amount of falling over, and a drinking game that led to one member of the group needing an ambulance and a stomach pump. By then, thank goodness, Azumi, Evan, Wendy and I were already back at our hotel – the heat, drink and jet lag finally catching up on our guests.

The next morning, more energetic than any of us had expected, we squeezed in a few more temples and shrines. While I'd grown a bit jaded with Kyoto after four visits, at least I knew the best places to go in order to avoid temple-fatigue (a well-known side effect of excessive sightseeing in the city, whereby every old wooden pagoda ends up looking the same as the last). We took in the simple Zen landscaping of Ginkakuji, the Silver Temple, with its perfectly raked pebble paths and gardens that included a replica of Mt Fuji sculpted from a pile of stones. Then we moved to Kiyomizudera, a more majestic structure clinging precariously to a hillside and overlooking some of the best kept streets in town. As we ambled down the narrow sloping street leading away from the temple, we stopped to sample the thick, green *maccha* tea (invigoratingly bitter) and the bean-paste-filled *yatsuhashi* snacks (invigoratingly sweet), then slurped up hot udon noodles and tempura for lunch.

As we neared the hotel, we noticed a small but refreshingly quiet temple and stopped to look around. The unmistakable Sunday afternoon pang of gloom was in the air. The sky had been overcast all day, trapping the humidity under the thick canopy cloud. But now the carefully-tended pebble garden began to rattle as the wind picked up and the grey above us turned to an angry black. Then the rain fell.

It seemed an unfair way to end an otherwise fantastic weekend, and it reminded me that Evan and Wendy would be leaving the next morning. The pitter-patter of water on rocks was in fact the opening movement of a harsh summer storm. We sheltered under the lip of the ornate tiled roof, the only visitors in this anonymous but pretty temple. Without umbrellas or rain jackets, we debated our options – make a mad wet dash for the hotel; or wait for the storm to pass but risk missing our bullet train back to Tokyo. We finally chose to stay put, and we fell into silence, protected by the roof, sitting on the terrace and watching the streaks of rain explode against the rocks and pebbles laid out in the garden. My opinion of the rain changed. It was melancholically beautiful, small streams forming in the tracks that had been sculpted that morning by the gardener, and entirely in keeping with my mix of joy and impending loss as I enjoyed these last few hours with my brother.

Ever the pragmatist, it was Azumi who finally spoke. We only had an hour to get back to the hotel, pick up our bags, and catch the *shinkansen*. We stood up, bracing ourselves for the inevitable soaking. Just as we did so, a shaven-headed monk appeared from the building behind us. He was carrying two large golf umbrellas.

'Keep them,' he said when we tried to politely refuse his offer, Azumi explaining that we were leaving Kyoto that day. 'You need them more than me.' He smiled and waved us on our way.

Thanks to the monk's generosity, we caught our train without the need for a change of clothes. Even in summer, it gets dark in Japan before seven p.m., and the rain-drenched night could have lent our final evening together a downbeat air. But as we sat next to our newly-acquired brollies and relived the highlights of the last few days, we enjoyed the food and drink in the carriage in far better spirits than I had expected. And our final farewell at Tokyo station hurt just a little less.

Television Was Watched by Me

My stomach was still in knots every time I taught with Ms Hasebe, never more so than when we were supposed to teach the third years the present perfect (for example, 'I haven't eaten dinner yet', 'I've already eaten dinner', 'I've just eaten dinner'). As usual I had prepared all of the required materials and suggested demonstrating the new language by having her enter the room first and say, 'Where's Garett? He hasn't arrived yet.' I would then come in and she would say, 'He has just arrived.' For any partially intelligent person this would be an easy task. But this was Hasebe.

We approached the classroom and I reminded her that I would wait just outside until after her first present perfect line. She said OK then walked into the room. Her usual inane blather in Japanese, the general theme being 'English is very difficult so you'll never be able to speak it, but try to learn a few things in order to scrape a pass in the high school entrance tests,' went on for a few minutes until she decided that teaching might be a good idea. 'OK, where's Garett?' So far, so good. 'Where's Garett?' Perhaps she was just confirming the question. 'Where's *Garett*?' This wasn't in the script. 'I said, where is GARETT?!' I was in the doorway but out of the students' line of vision, and Hasebe looked at me angrily. I gestured maniacally and mouthed, 'He hasn't arrived yet.' It didn't register and she became quite agitated, finally shouting at me in front of the open-mouthed students. 'Garett, what are you doing?! Come in now!' I stepped inside, eyebrow raised but unable to do anything else in case I ended up looking as unprofessional as her. She tried to regain her composure. 'Right. You haven't arrived yet.' Then to the class, 'Garett hasn't arrived yet.' They looked at me, I looked at them and I didn't know whether to laugh or cry.

'I've just arrived.'

After further demonstrations, when I managed to wrestle control of the situation from her, I wanted to involve the students by having them make similar sentences. 'No, no, they can't do it,' Hasebe said, just as they were doing it. 'Let me explain.' As usual she then began a half-hour explanation of the grammar almost entirely in Japanese, and copied out the long explanation from her teacher's manual onto the blackboard, the kids in turn copying that into their exercise books. The emphasis in language education in Japan was too grammar-focused at the best of times (the Ministry of Education's promises to promote communicative, real-life use of English completely at odds with the multiple choice, grammar-centric exams that they set) but Hasebe took it to a whole new level of tedium. She would use three colours of chalk to highlight the separate components of a sentence, and arrows and plus signs would fly in every direction until a sentence such as 'I have just seen my friend' ended up resembling a mathematical equation. The few students still awake and not too busy reading *manga* would write these notes then file them away, probably never to be seen again. The swotty kids would be able to bandy around terms such as 'past participle' and 'verb conjunctions' with frightening ease, but be wholly unaware of when and why we actually *use* any of these structures. After a month of lessons on passive voice, one of the best students was able to use it brilliantly, just not appropriately: 'Garett, television was watched by me last night. Then curry was eaten by my family.'

'Wow! Good English is spoken by you.'

Ms Hasebe didn't seem to care whether the students understood or not, just as long as we completed the textbook page by the end of the lesson so that we could move on to the next point. I never really understood why she always seemed in such a hurry to race through the chapters, even when students complained that we were moving too fast, because it resulted in us finishing too soon then having to think of new ways to fill the unplanned lessons. More truthfully, *I* had to think of new ways to fill the unplanned lessons, creating worksheet upon worksheet and receiving little or no thanks. Whenever I suggested giving the students an opportunity to actually speak, to really use the language properly, Hasebe would resort to her tired refrain: 'The kids are stupid.' Or, even better, 'No, that's boring for them.' So, instead of doing dull things like speaking to one another, the students got to while away the hour with another thrilling fill-the-gap exercise. But at least it made life easier for Ms Hasebe.

Ms Maki was hired in order to split second and third year classes in two, she teaching one half while Ms Hasebe or Ms Ikuta taught the other; I would act as the assistant to alternating groups. This seemed a fantastic opportunity, the kids learning in classes of just fifteen students with one or two teachers to help them learn. For Ms Ikuta's second years this was indeed the case and in the relaxed but focused atmosphere of small classes the students got more chance to speak, more personal attention and, eventually, higher grades. Disappointingly, yet expectedly, Ms Hasebe used Ms Maki's arrival to improve her own situation. Unbeknownst to the Principal or Vice-Principal, she had Ms Maki teach the whole class single-handedly or in tandem with me, while Hasebe could take it easy in the staffroom. In the very seniority-based work culture, Ms Maki, as the new part-timer (the term used loosely; like me, she taught more classes than many so-called full-timers, just got less money), didn't feel comfortable complaining, but it was disgraceful that taxpayers were funding an extra teacher in order to raise the standard of their children's education but Hasebe was using it to give herself a few extra coffee breaks. I suppose, on a positive note, this indirectly helped the children as Ms Maki's lessons were a lot more informative and interesting, and there were fewer moments of comedy confusion with Ms Hasebe out of the way.

I much preferred working with Ms Maki as her ideas on teaching were similar to mine. She believed that the key to confident language use was through speaking and that an over-emphasis on grammar was counter-productive. Unfortunately Hasebe, despite not bothering to show up for half of the lessons, insisted Ms Maki follow her instructions so the changes were small – but noticeable.

Irritatingly, a few students complained that Ms Maki was too strict. This was because she actually suggested that the students participate in the lessons, which, after two years of sleeping, chatting and drawing in class, came as a great shock to some of them. I saw Ms Hasebe's nasty side as she revelled in the students' complaints and shamelessly exaggerated the details of incidents, forgetting that I had been present at the time: 'Ms Maki hit Ohara kun,' she whispered to me, feigning outrage.

'No she didn't.'

'And she used the 'F' word with him.'

'No, she didn't. I was there.'

'Well, she said it in Japanese.'

There is no Japanese equivalent to the 'F' word, but I knew that would be a pointless argument, so I stuck to the facts: 'She just told him to be quiet after he was mean to another student.'

'Ohara says she's making a bad atmosphere in the classroom.'

'Ohara's been making a bad atmosphere all term. He was just upset because someone finally had the guts to tell him off.'

'If you see her do anything like that again, you must tell me. It's not good for the school.'

I had seen her act similarly earlier in the year. One of her old students said something derogatory about Ms Ikuta and, rather than tell the girl not to be rude, she dug for more information. It transpired that the student was just annoyed because Ms Ikuta wouldn't let her read a comic during English class, but Ms Hasebe

133

deliberately stirred things up by asking if Ms Ikuta had done anything else to upset her. The girl couldn't think of anything but Hasebe kept pushing, desperate for dirt and keen to make it clear that she was so much nicer than any other teacher. It betrayed an insecure nature, someone in need of the students' friendship, when it's a teacher's job to be approachable but – as hard as it sounds – *not* their friend. Ironically, the same girl later became very keen on Ms Ikuta, and the students clearly respected her consistency and fairness whereas Ms Hasebe's attempts to be a surrogate big sister contributed to the near-total state of anarchy in her lessons. The kids smelled weakness and duly took advantage.

It took time, too, for Ms Maki to win the third year students over after they had become so used to treating English class as an extension of break time, but they came round eventually. As disgusting as it was that Hasebe was skiving at the expense of the students, it quite possibly saved their English education.

Skimpy Sumo-Style Underpants

With the temperature increasing every day and the humidity sucking the air and enthusiasm out of every pupil, it was a relief to approach the long summer holiday at last. It would be a chance to relax, meet friends (in a city the size of Tokyo it's easy to suddenly find it's been six months without having seen some of my closest mates) and catch up on my Master's degree study, which had been slipping terribly in recent months.

Summer, too, is *matsuri* season in Japan – the summer festival. On almost any night of the week, I could stand on the balcony of my flat and hear the fierce rhythms of the *taiko* drums, or strange, pleasing melodies from penny whistles. Most of these festivals would centre around a local shrine, and the highlight was carrying the *mikoshi* around the neighbourhood. This *mikoshi* is a heavy palanquin with a small portable shrine on top, and – depending on the size – groups of ten or fifty people hoist them on their shoulders and bob them up and down to the beat of the drums. While doing this, wearing a short summer kimono and daringly skimpy sumo-style underpants, the group chants and sings to the thousands of bystanders, who throw buckets of water at them. I had actually participated in such an event when I'd lived in Oyama and, far from being a nuisance, the water was welcome relief in the stifling heat, washing away the sweat and splinters. There was a real sense of camaraderie as we heaved the massive *mikoshi* for hours on our shoulders, until we could return it to its permanent home in the shrine. There, we collapsed on the ground and enjoyed *bento* lunchboxes of fish and rice, sipped bottomless cups of *sake*, and iced our sore shoulders. I woke the next day with exposed privates, a screaming hangover, and a purple bruise that lasted till autumn.

Now, though, I could enjoy the events as an onlooker. Not only were there *mikoshi* parades to watch, but also various displays of music and dancing – from the most traditional kimono-clad rituals to rockabilly and hip-hop. By far the most popular show was the samba, when a mass of middle-aged men with zoom-lens cameras suddenly gathered in front of the stage to watch the twenty-something women shimmy in sequined bikinis. It was heartening to see such appreciation for the Latin American arts among the local male population.

There were copious amounts of street food. Fried noodles, omelettes and potatoes, chocolate-covered bananas, and *kaki gori* – flavoured shaved ice – which was a favourite among local kids who got to mix their own cocktail of E-number-filled syrup.

The summer festival, of course, is not unique to Japan, but I have rarely seen such devotion to the event elsewhere. It's often crowded and messy, and *matsuri* are known to have dubious connections to the yakuza (as do many shrine-related activities, especially if they generate a lot of business). Indeed, in my neighbourhood, there was suddenly a far higher proportion of men with punch perms and ornate tattoos peeking out from under their baggy tracksuit tops (the yakuza uniform seemingly paying homage to *The Sopranos*). But it is also a family event, with every generation mingling, many wearing brightly-coloured *yukata* summer kimono; everyone eating, drinking, and joining the community o*bon* dance.

The three-day festival near my school celebrated the area's fishing tradition, with special dances based on ancient fishermen's actions, and the majority of stalls selling octopus and scallops.

Azumi came to join me one evening, and the students were amazed to see me outside school, and… with a woman! Poor Azumi had a far harder time than I did as she put up with groups of teenagers staring and whispering to one another, then the more confident kids approaching and peppering her with questions. I could laugh at her obvious embarrassment, until they asked 'When are you getting married?' At this point I would be distracted by an especially interesting candy floss stall.

It was great, though, to see the students outside the usual school environment, and not wearing their dark navy uniforms. And it was interesting how much more relaxed they appeared, many happy to try out their burgeoning English skills without fear of mistake – something I rarely saw at school with its more rigid results-based culture.

The evening after that festival, Azumi and I attended the Sumida River Fireworks – one of the largest events of its kind. The Sumida River runs through the old heart of Tokyo and is now flanked by apartment blocks and office buildings. The centre for these fireworks is Ryogoku, next to the main sumo stadium, lending it a traditional air, and – just like at the *matsuri* – many of the one million people in the audience wear *yukata* or *happi*, the traditional summer wear.

Unfortunately, with so many tall buildings and bridges now squeezed into the district, it was very difficult to find a suitable viewing spot. The custom at these fireworks displays (known, poetically, in Japanese as *hanabi* – 'flower fire') is for someone in the group to go early, sometimes even days before, tape down some cardboard or tarpaulin with their name written on it, and claim a position. I was both awed at the level of trust and community-spirit required for this system to work (there was nothing stopping someone from moving these markers, or writing their own name over someone else's), but also slightly irritated. As Azumi and I walked and walked, desperate to find a spot as the starting time neared, we saw swathes of empty space – but nobody filled it because it was covered in blue sheets and masking tape. Never mind that these people may not be coming, and never mind that thousands of spectators were forced to squeeze into tiny pockets of unclaimed land – the rules must be followed at all costs. Even Azumi, usually looser than most with these kinds of things, was reticent to sit on a square of blue tarpaulin, despite it being unused even as the first flashes exploded in the air.

As with so many Japanese events, drinking plays a huge part. We had brought a six-pack to see us through the hour-and-fifteen-minutes of 'flower fire'. It was getting warm by now, but it was still pleasant to sip beer and watch the rockets dances and sparkle. This was nothing like the Guy Fawkes Nights back home, when each firework would go up one-by-one, the whole thing lasting perhaps twenty minutes punctured with breaks. This display was a nearly unbreakable cacophony of fizzing light in time to the music, with pictures of cartoon characters created in the sky and Tokyo's nightline illuminated by the full spectrum of colours. I have often laughed at the Japanese propensity for tears, but as I saw eyes glisten red and green and silver, I felt myself becoming emotional. It was such a visceral sensation, the whole body shaking to the blasts and crackles.

Then I looked to my left. Azumi was sobbing.

'What's the matter?' I asked. I was half-joking, aware that so many around us were similarly moved by the stunning display. 'Are you happy or sad?'

She turned away a moment, then looked back at me.

'I don't know.'

Terminal

'Garett. Grandma's ill.' It was my dad on the phone. 'It's leukaemia,' he added. 'Terminal.'

The next few weeks were the summer holiday, but I felt very little joy as my family updated me daily on my grandmother's swift deterioration. While I was accustomed to my self-induced exile making for sad farewells and joyful reunions, it had not occurred to me that it would also distance me from loved ones as they battled for their lives. Of course there was nothing anyone could have done – the diagnosis came too late, deeming treatment useless – but there's a specific kind of helplessness at being thousands of miles away as the realisation dawned: Grandma was dying. This powerful, cheerful, wonderful woman, who had never seemed old to me (she loved football and science-fiction films, for goodness sake!) was now reaching the end of her life.

I should have gone home, but Grandma forbade me, insisting that I save my money and go back for a happier occasion. I should have spoken to her more often on the phone, but – it shames me to say it – I struggled for words when I talked to her, tripping over every sentence as I worried too much about saying the wrong thing.

Before the school holiday finished, she was gone.

Like in the UK education system, the Japanese summer vacation lasts for about six weeks and usually it's a welcome time to try and relax and stay cool. Best of all, I could avoid the stifling heat and humidity of the daily commute in shirt and tie, instead fanning myself at home in t-shirt and shorts. But at this time, with my heart broken and filled with regret, I wished I could go to work. Instead, I stewed in my sadness and self-loathing. Why hadn't I called Grandma more often before she was ill? And why hadn't I called her more after she was diagnosed? The answer was simple: because I was selfish and a coward.

Back when I was working at the conversation school in Tochigi prefecture, I conducted a lesson using childhood memories to practise storytelling skills. I had expected it to be an enjoyable exercise and I looked forward to hearing my students reminisce, misty-eyed, about their youth. I started things off by telling them about the football team I founded with my brother when we were eleven, and our plucky runners-up display in our first ever tournament. I could have gone on all day with descriptions of our club's fluid passing style and a blow-by-blow account of the epic see-saw encounter with our nearest rivals – the local private school, no less – but thought it might be good for the students to speak a bit, so I opened the floor. Fumiko talked about climbing the local mountain with her family and eating rice balls filled with salmon as she lazed in the grass and looked down on the city; Junko remembered seeing a snake cross her path on her morning walk to school and her sister crying with fright; Nobuko told us about joining a tennis camp with her friends and their excitement at staying in a dormitory.

'Takashi, how about you?'

Takashi was in his eighties, a retired high school teacher of world history who had decided to take up studying English relatively late in life, partly to aid him on his trips abroad with his wife, but primarily to stretch himself and to keep his mind as healthy as his body (as well as being an avid gardener, he woke up early every day to take an hour-long walk along the river). He had progressed quickly in English, a natural curiosity and will to communicate pushing him to study hard and practise constantly. I was genuinely interested in his tales of childhood but, contrary to his usual gregariousness, he held back. 'My childhood wasn't very interesting. We didn't take any holidays.'

'That's OK. Do you have any smaller memories? About school? About your friends? Anything is OK.'

'Well, I do remember one thing very clearly.'

'Please.' The other students' ears pricked up.

'I remember seeing the town of Ashikaga flashing with lights. I thought they were fireworks, but they were bombs. It was an American raid. It was so loud and so hot.'

Obviously, I've met many people who have lived through the War, with stories to tell or experiences they'd rather forget: my maternal grandfather flew Lancaster bombers and saw almost every one of his friends die as they crashed into the English Channel; my paternal grandfather fought the Japanese in Burma, barely seeing his child, my dad, for the first five years of his life. But to hear this

142

simple, harrowing description from somebody on the other side of the world divide at the time was very affecting. I was even more impressed by the way Takashi had seen such sights but was now dedicating himself to studying the language of the old enemy, fascinated about the cultures of the English-speaking world.

The school was run on a free-booking system where students were able to arrange lesson times as they wished. This made for a hectic but varied schedule, with teachers unsure who they would be teaching until the start of their shift. But Takashi was a creature of habit and, along with a small hardcore, became a Friday morning regular. I relied on him to keep me updated on the latest Japanese rugby news – he was a die-hard supporter of his old university team, Waseda – while he would ask me about the comings and goings in the European game, forcing me to review the BBC website every evening just in case my knowledge should come into question. Despite being deep into retirement Takashi was always immaculately dressed, his tie perfectly centred over a fastened top button, his suit jacket only coming off in the height of summer (much to my discomfort, Oyama was in one of the hottest areas of mainland Japan, with August temperatures sometimes hitting forty degrees celsius and heavy humidity blanketing the city). His clothing suited his personality well, a gentleman and gentle man who became a firm favourite with his classmates on Fridays, most of whom were housewives, both in the lessons and afterwards in their regular coffee shop visits.

The most controversial of the many rules of the school was

the ban on teachers socialising with students. The rule was supposedly designed to protect both sides from misunderstandings or awkward situations, but actually caused more strife than it solved. When students registered they were asked to explain why they wanted to study English; a vast majority said it was because they wanted to make friends with foreigners. And when teachers joined the company most expressed an interest in getting to know Japanese people better. But the teachers were forbidden from any kind of relationship with the students outside the forty-minute lessons. Whether the rule was introduced with good intentions or not, it was a violation of basic rights and against the wishes of students and teachers. And when Takashi said he would love to watch a rugby game with me, I had to risk my job or decline. So I risked my job, but felt a knot in my stomach whenever I heard him mention rugby to any other teacher, for fear that my secret liaisons with this lovely old man would cause a scandal.

Thankfully, the cloak and dagger precautions could end when I left for my new job in a different conversation school in Tokyo. Every couple of months I would meet Takashi and his daughters at Shinanomachi station in central Tokyo, then follow the crowds to the old Olympic complex where the ugly, concrete bowl of a National Stadium overshadowed the smaller but more aesthetically-pleasing Chichibunomiya Stadium. This was a rugby-specific little chocolate box of a ground, the touchlines just a couple of metres from the front row of seats, creating a warm, intimate atmosphere where the thump of every tackle reverberated through the concrete. Usually we watched Waseda University take on and beat all-comers on their way to another Championship, the spectators an equal mix of college students, 'OBs' (the Japanese using the English acronym for 'Old Boys' – a nod to their age and their status as alumni of one of Japan's most prestigious universities) and young families enjoying the emphatic victory. The demographic altered only slightly for national team and Top League games, the shouting becoming more raucous as the varsity crowd were joined by more casual fans, and the results were less predictable.

Takashi talked warmly of his wife, another retired teacher with a busy schedule of hobbies and gardening, but to me she became like one of those characters in sit-coms who we never actually see – Norm's wife Vera in *Cheers!* or 'Er Indoors from *Minder*. Apparently she never caught the rugby bug that Takashi transmitted to his daughters but she still contributed to our days by producing lunchboxes full of homemade snacks. These rice balls and biscuits were accompanied by cups of warm *sake*, the most effective protection against the cold I've ever come across, the warmth spreading slowly and comfortably through the body.

Our friendship wasn't limited solely to sport, and often we would meet just for lunch and a few drinks – Takashi always insisting on paying – and a chance to catch up on the latest gossip from Takashi's life in Tochigi and mine in Tokyo.

When I received an e-mail from him on the train home from school, still reeling from Grandma's news, I presumed it was to plan another meeting soon. Takashi's English was excellent but, understandably, lacked the subtlety of nuance one would expect from a native speaker. The message was direct and terrifyingly clear: 'Garett, I have cancer in my colon.'

Most of the time I cruise through life, able to convince myself that the really bad things only happen to other people or at other times. Death and disease aren't supposed to be for the here and now; they're things to contemplate from a safe distance, not deal with in their physical state. When, as is inevitable, those distant people and times turn out to be me and my family – right now – it's as if I'm suddenly exposed, open to further attack, no longer protected by the odds that usually run in my favour. After Grandma's news, Takashi's was somehow more likely.

Unlike Grandma, Takashi's cancer was at least beatable – and he was admitted to hospital for an operation. All I could do, all anyone could do, was give him our best wishes, cross every finger, and wait.

A Detective Who is Actually a Dog in Human Form

As the summer days stretched out, my ennui – and faulty internet – prevented me from doing anything constructive. Instead, I found myself watching more and more television. In most parts of the world, this would probably be a test for a person's patience, but in Japan I'm surprised that it's not the cause of more murders or suicides. Different cultures have different expectations of their mass media, of course, and clearly there are certain kinds of entertainment that lend themselves better to some countries than others. But Japanese TV is absolutely, unequivocally awful.

When I tell friends back home about how bad the programmes are, they usually respond with something like, 'Well, things are pretty poor here; there's hardly anything I watch these days.' What they don't realise is that even the worst British TV show will be made with a certain amount of care and attention. Take any daytime quiz or reality programme and you can imagine that the people involved are at least trying to do the best they can with the materials available. But the level of expectation is so low in Japan that one feels the producers are laughing all the way to the bank, aware that they can get away with putting pretty much anything on screen – *and the audience will not care.*

Essentially, there are two kinds of programme on the main

channels: drama and 'variety'. The term drama is used very loosely to mean any fictional story, almost always based on a manga, and generally lacking any discernible drama whatsoever. The sheer volume of famous people in the country is mind-boggling, with all-powerful talent agencies pushing their latest finds onto the TV studios, making deals that will allow a new drama to use the agency's hottest established stars just as long as they also employ a certain number of the lesser-known members from their stable. These lower-ranking starlets then get exposure on primetime shows, ensuring that they become fully-fledged stars in their own right, thus perpetuating the cycle, making the agencies ever more powerful and giving them the leverage to push even more up-and-comers into future shows. While this whiffs of corruption – the same handful of agencies effectively running the entire TV industry – it shouldn't have any great impact on the quality of the shows. Surely, in order to be represented by the big agencies, a young actor would need to be pretty good at their job… But not in Japan.

I met an actor once as I participated in a promotional photo shoot for my previous conversation school. He was charismatic, handsome and engaging, and he worked steadily in the theatre, as well as winning some small roles in independent feature films. But when I asked him, 'Have you ever appeared on TV?' he looked at me, perplexed.

'No. I can't.'

'Can't?' It was my turn to be confused.

'Yeah, I'm an actor.'

'Right. So…'

'I'm not in one of the agencies.' He shrugged, like it was obvious.

'But don't they watch your plays? Don't they try to represent people like you?'

He laughed out loud and shook his head. 'No, no. That's for idols.'

Idols.

Unlike my understanding of the word, in which someone has to earn that label based on an impressive body of work and a devoted fan following, in Japan the term is applied to young wannabe pop stars, usually in their early teens, who are groomed for stardom by these slightly shady agencies based solely on looks. They are then sent out to perform as singers, models, event staff, dancers – in any shopping mall or small-scale festival that will take them. The philosophy seems to be that if they throw enough shit at the wall, eventually something will stick. The agency keeps the majority of these young people's payment for themselves (in return for the faint promise of fame), jettisons those who don't become stars before they finish puberty, then continues pushing the few successes into dramas and commercials.

The unfairness of the situation is out there for everyone to see, but in true Japanese style most people choose to ignore it. The potential for abuse, with the balance so heavily in the power of the agent over the performer, has led to rumours of parts being exchanged for sexual favours and complaints of unfair dismissal which always disappear disturbingly quickly.

But for the audience, the most striking result of this fixed system is that real actors get sidelined in theatre and barely-watched films, while the mainstream media is packed full of 'actors' who simply cannot act. The Japanese work ethic is renowned throughout the world – businesses are built on a worker-bee philosophy; if a kid wants to be a baseball star, he will practise for hour and hours, every day, every week. Yet, in the closed shop of Japanese TV there appears to be no motivation to try hard, no reason to learn and hone the craft. In fact, the young stars appear in so many programmes, movies and commercials that they probably have no time to even stop and reflect on their performance before they're preparing for a new role. So a primetime drama ostensibly aimed at adults will contain acting that would be considered below-par and hammy in a primary school play. If someone is supposed to show that their character is hungry, they will emote this by rubbing their tummy theatrically and saying, slowly and deliberately, 'I… am… hungry,' as if talking to a hard-of-hearing three-year-old who doesn't speak the language. If they are angry, they will pull the stock bad-boy snarl (the lip curled up at one side) and elongate the last syllable of every sentence. If they are in love, they will put a hand on their heart, sigh dreamily and give a moony grin. And this takes place in shaky, balsa wood sets, and costumes that still bear the creases of being fresh out of their packaging; all accompanied by the kind of soundtrack that will happily go 'Wah, wah, waaaahh' after every moment of humour.

It genuinely flummoxes me how this mediocrity is allowed to

continue. The great Japanese public has access to Hollywood films and, to a lesser extent, TV dramas. They must be able to see that in comparison to the polished American product, their version is cringeworthily horrendous, but anyone I talk to about it simply shrugs their shoulders as if to say, 'Well, yeah… but what do you expect?'

Similarly, the so-called 'variety' programmes suffer from the same dearth of genuine skill or care. Just as the dramas lack drama, so variety lacks any variety. They will generally feature a panel of unfunny and untalented 'talent' (a feature of all Japanese TV is the number of ironic misnomers – drama, variety, talent) reacting to… well, not much. It's usually video footage of someone eating some food, or visiting a small town in Japan (which is always mind-blowingly amazing to every member of the panel) or a foreign country (which is always stunningly weird in its non-Japanese-ness). Everyone will react in unison with utter amazement ('Ehhhh!') or shock ('Ehhhh?') at what they are witnessing, and no-one will say anything that does not conform with what everybody else has been told to think. One show included a feature from the Netherlands in which a supposed local penchant for reusing materials and saving electricity was the main focus. The Japanese wife of a Dutchman bemoaned the fact that he would always turn off the lights when he left the room or try to use a toothbrush for as long as possible before disposing of it. She said he was cheap, and this then became the mantra uttered by every participant in the programme – 'Dutch people are so cheap!' At no time did anyone stop to say that they were basing this stereotype on the actions of just one person from Holland, and nobody thought to mention that these habits could also be seen as ecologically friendly. No, it was so much more fun for all involved to keep repeating 'Dutch people are so cheap' for the rest of the segment.

Worst of all, from my point of view, was that in that long, strange summer, I struggled to drag myself away. I couldn't focus on books, Japanese study or my Master's (I was supposed to be completing my thesis); I'd exhausted my DVD collection, and my lack of internet prevented me from downloading any other films or podcasts. Most shamefully of all, I started deriving a perverse sense of pleasure from the sheer atrociousness of the television on offer. Like when you tickle an itch before scratching it, or dare yourself not to turn away from a gruesome scene in a horror film, I would try to see just how much I could take before I had to switch off. I even started devising little contests, making personal bets on whether this next programme could be even worse than the one before, or challenging myself to watch five minutes of the drama about a detective who is actually a dog in human form (a programme aimed at grown-ups) without making any audible noise of disapproval.

I lost, in so many ways.

Look at His Tall Nose

Alongside deepening my knowledge of mind-numbing television, I spent much of the summer exploring that other way of destroying brain cells – alcohol.

My previous job had been in a conversation school, and, as a large proportion of students were businesspeople, then the busiest time of day would be in the evening. The 'salaryman' or 'office lady' would finish their day's work in central Tokyo, then come to practise English for an hour or two, some for fun, some in preparation for overseas trips, and some because their companies told them to. This schedule had meant that I would usually finish my day around nine thirty p.m., at a time when it almost seemed rude not to go for a drink with my colleagues.

One of the reasons for changing to my junior high school job with its more conventional hours was to break the cycle of just working, drinking, sleeping late – then repeating. Until now, my new routine had suited me well – I'd been studying more, exercising regularly, eating better and drinking less. But during the summer vacation, I slipped back into old habits. Most of my non-Japanese friends were still working at conversation schools, so on any given evening I could find someone who was up for a few beers.

When I had first arrived in Japan and lived in rural Tochigi prefecture, I had prided myself on embracing the local culture, drinking at independent little *izakaya* bars and avoiding falling into the *gaijin* culture. On the occasional trip down to Tokyo I had pitied the Westerners who knew only the American-style bars or mock British pubs – it seemed such a waste of the opportunity to try new things. But since coming to Tokyo, I had slowly drifted into that lifestyle, at least when I was out with certain circles of friends. There were benefits to this. For starters, international bars would at least let customers pay separately rather than share a tab – something that made life a lot less complicated at the end of a drunken night. There was also something quite comforting in being surrounded by people who shared similar experiences – the joys and frustrations of being a foreigner, especially an English teacher, in Japan. It must also be said that… there were women.

There's no doubt that my social capital had gone up by being a Caucasian male in Japan. Immediately after arriving at Narita Airport, I realised that I stood out in a crowd – fair-haired and blue-eyed in a largely homogenous population. As arrogant as it sounds, I soon became quite used to people looking at me, and – as for many Japanese the idea of a foreigner speaking the language is unthinkable – hearing compliments about my looks: 'He's so cool!' or 'Look at his tall nose!' (In Japan, this is considered a good thing, though I'm not entirely sure what it means.) While hearing these compliments was undeniably pleasant at first, I soon realised that it was also quite superficial. Once again, it's difficult to talk about this without sounding conceited, but it's a bit like how I imagine life is for a mid-ranking movie actor – people are occasionally surprised and happy to see you, they may excitedly utter a few words to you, or even ask for a photo (yes, that really happens), but they rarely see past your façade – the *idea* of you as a celebrity (or a white person in Japan) being more important to them than the real person.

Having been in a reltationship since arriving in the country, I could feel partially frustrated – why am I suddenly a sought-after commodity now that I'm attached?! – but also quite relaxed about the situation, able to enjoy the minor attention but not get my head turned too much. The same could not be said about all of my Western friends, and these *gaijin* bars acted as magnets both for foreigners and for locals interested in foreigners. I always thought that it made more sense to go to a bar where there were *not* tons of other Western men vying for the girls' attention; but this never seemed to bother most of my companions. The admittedly sensible argument was that in a local *izakaya*, everyone would be sat at tables and, for the most part, it was not the done thing to go and talk to another group. But in a sports bar or Irish pub, then everyone was standing, moving around and more open to meeting new people.

My regular drinking buddy was Stevie, an affable Liverpudlian and the most gifted linguist I've ever met. In fact, it would frustrate the hell out of me how I would invest hours and hours into studying Japanese and be delighted if I remembered one or two new words a week, but if Stevie heard a new phrase once, just in passing, then it would immediately be locked away in his head, available for him to recycle later in conversation – and with no apparent effort whatsoever. Naturally, this ability to spout local colloquialisms helped his popularity with the natives and, while he enjoyed a lot of success with females, he would be equally happy making friends with both sexes, so on many an occasion we would end up in a karaoke booth with a university baseball team or cabal of business executives. And these parties would stretch way beyond the one a.m. cut-off for my last train.

We've already established that my girlfriend was a patient person and, being someone who could drink me under the table at times, Azumi was not averse to the occasional all-night drinking session herself. However, as my late-night texted apologies became more and more frequent, and as I stumbled in at seven in the morning – just as she was getting ready for work – for the third or fourth time in a week, the situation became less and less tolerable. I was aware of this, and – drunk and sentimental – I would vow to change my ways. Then one or two days later, I would do it again.

These nights would start with the best intentions. After a day cooped up under the air-conditioner and stewing in sweat, sadness and bad TV, I'd go and meet Stevie and other friends in central Tokyo, just for a couple of pints. The problem was that after these couple of pints, my ability to make sensible decisions began to diminish. And then, as the time of the last train fast approached (in that funny way that time speeds up the drunker one gets), I would be enjoying myself more and more, and… deep down, I kind of *wanted* to miss that train. At this point we'd be going to another bar, probably chatting to random strangers and thinking about heading to the night clubs of Roppongi – the slightly seedy but decidedly lively centre of Tokyo hedonism. Dodging the grasps of African doormen sometimes physically trying to drag us into hostess bars, and the equally persistent efforts of Chinese women in thick winter jackets whispering 'Massage, massage' into our ears, we toured the half-dozen most crowded clubs. And – oh, the shame – I enjoyed the attention of beautiful women who wanted to meet this exotic fair-haired foreigner, to talk to me, dance with me, and possibly do other things with me. To my very minor credit, I was able to resist the very real temptation of a one-night stand, but there's no doubt that I also enjoyed the ego boost I received every time one of these women showed interest, however superficial it may have been.

Azumi was not stupid. She knew what went on in Roppongi, she could smell the scent of other women on me. My protestations that 'nothing happened,' while technically true, were of no comfort to her as she would lose sleep and text me at three a.m. to ask where I was. And in my drunken, messed-up state, I would use these late-night messages as evidence of Azumi's possessiveness, thus justifying my actions, however unfairly. I was having a tough time, I would tell myself, I was on holiday. I *deserved* to cut loose and have some fun for a few weeks.

In the end, I was caught out by the biggest cliché of all. It was early September, just as school had re-started for the autumn trimester. At the end of my first week back at work, and still reeling from the loss of Grandma and Takashi's news, I went out for a start-of-term party with some of the teachers. It was a pleasant but low-key affair in the swanky Ginza neighbourhood: French food in small but expensive portions, and Pinot Noir of – I was told – an especially rare vintage. On another night I may have enjoyed a taste of the good life, but on this occasion I was restless, filled with a nervous energy. So, as everyone began to disperse at the train station, I called Stevie and arranged to meet up with him and some other ex-workmates for a drink in Roppongi.

As had become the norm, this drink led to another, and another, until dawn broke over Tokyo. I had been in one of the cavernous underground clubs, somehow becoming separated from my friends. Not to worry, I'd decided, as a group of nurses on a birthday party soon took me under their wing. We danced and drank until the first train of the morning, I gave the chattiest girl a hug goodbye, and I arrived home just as Azumi was eating breakfast. She looked at my white shirt collar and asked what the red smear was. I guessed that it was from a shaving cut the previous day.

A few minutes later, I saw the mark as I undressed. It was larger than expected from what I had thought was a small nick of the razor on my neck. I scrubbed the shirt with my hands, machine washed it… but the stain wouldn't come out. So I took it to the lovely old ladies at the local dry cleaners'.

Two days later, I picked up my shirt, cleaned, pressed and packaged. There was a spidery, scrawled note in Japanese on the wrapping that I couldn't decipher. I thought nothing of it as I tossed it on the bed and started making dinner.

Azumi came home from work, went to get changed in the bedroom, and found the wrapped shirt. She brought it to me in the kitchen, and translated the note:

Lipstick on collar. Could not remove.

No Pets, No Foreigners

As a kid, I remember talking with some friends about what kind of things we would find if we went to hell. I think the list included things like Brussels sprouts, itchy woollen jumpers, and triple maths lessons every day. Now I know a new corner of Hades: the Japanese estate agent.

I entered the office to be greeted by a pair of men in shabby suits. The older and rounder of them was smoking greedily, while his weasel-faced, unshaven junior hastily put his tie on – *over* shirt his collar. They looked vaguely annoyed at my appearance but the plumper of the two struggled to remember his manners, stubbed out his cigarette and offered me a seat.

He asked what I was looking for and I gave him my very simple wish list: somewhere small and reasonably priced, within ten minutes' walk of the station. He sucked air through his yellow teeth, and his partner chuckled knowingly.

'That will be difficult.'

'Difficult? Why?'

'Well...' He looked me up and down. 'Is it just for *you*?'

'Yes.'

'Are you single?' This felt like a low blow. I'd been single for less than twenty-four hours, which was why I was here, looking for a new flat.

'Yes. I'm… single.' The word caught on my throat a bit. The younger man (we'll call him Weasel), pretending to busy himself at the back of the shop, laughed again, this time louder. 'Will that be a problem?' I asked innocently. In truth, I already knew where this conversation was going. I'd searched for apartments in Japan before.

'Many of the building owners don't rent to foreigners.'

'But that's illegal,' I protested. Weasel snorted, knowing full well that it's a law that is utterly ignored by all parties. In fact, I had previously complained to the police about similar treatment when barred from entering a hotel due to my foreign-ness. The officers found that situation similarly hilarious. It's funny how, while most rules in Japan are followed at all costs, even if they are completely illogical, the laws regarding discrimination towards non-Japanese are shrugged off as merely guidelines.

Mr Plump sighed. 'Can you speak Japanese?' It's amazing how often I'm asked that question – having spent the entire conversation up to that point speaking to a person solely in Japanese. I responded as politely as possible. As galling as this was, I knew that they held all the power, and I needed to find a place to live as soon as possible. 'Well… We'll see what we can do…'

We proceeded to search through floor plans and photos in a fat ring binder, estate agents being as stubbornly low-tech as so many Japanese institutions, where the fax machine is still a fixture in most offices. When we stopped on a page that looked interesting, I occasionally noticed a piece of small print in the Terms and Conditions: *No pets, no foreigners.*

Other pages didn't have that note, but Mr Plump would shake his head, Weasel would smirk, and we would move on. Occasionally we found a place that looked promising and whose owner was *not* known to be actively xenophobic. The estate agent called them and had a hushed conversation that always included the words *foreigner, British,* and the rather desperate addition, 'But he can speak some Japanese.' Most of these conversations ended abruptly, but occasionally Mr Plump would persuade them that I was not a terrible monster who would burn the building down. After three hours, we managed to find a grand total of two potential places willing to take a chance on someone from overseas.

After checking these out, I swiftly chose the one I wanted. Time was of the essence and, anyway, it wasn't as if I was spoiled for choice. I hoped we would sort it all out so that I could move in within a few days.

Back in the estate agents' office, we began filling out the forms required to get the flat. A high proportion of young people in Japan stay at home with their parents until marrying. It's easy to see why – it's just so much *effort* to rent a place. The form required full details of my job and salary, plus a certificate from my employers to tell them how long I'd been working there. It asked for my parents' names and addresses, two pieces of I.D., and the contact details of at least two people who could vouch for who I was (and these people could not be foreign, naturally).

The form asked for the reason why I had left my previous abode. I told Mr Plump that it was personal and I'd rather not say, but he insisted it was required, otherwise I would not be able to move in. I took a breath, swallowed hard, then spoke:

'Umm, I was living with my girlfriend, but we broke up.' This brought howls of laughter from Mr Plump and Weasel.

'Find another girlfriend, did you?' Mr Plump asked with a sly grin, clearly thinking I would enjoy this conspiratorial exchange.

'I'd rather not talk about it,' I muttered.

The form then asked for the name of my previous cohabitant. When I wrote it down, both Mr Plump and Weasel leaned forward to read it.

'Azumi,' Weasel leered. 'Pretty name.' I was genuinely speechless, and all I could do was give him a look that said *Really?* The insane thing was, I think he actually thought he was being friendly.

Mr Plump and I continued working through the form together and it said that they needed a copy of my family register, an official piece of paper that every Japanese family had, but – of course – I did not.

'I have a passport.'

'Not good enough,' Weasel replied with a sneer. I think he was willing to pass up a commission just so long as he could piss me off.

'I have my Japanese resident card.' This is a photo I.D. provided by the government proving that I had the right to live and work in Japan.

'Not good enough. You must show us a copy of your family

register.'

'But it's impossible for me to get a family register, because I'm not a member of any Japanese family.'

'Well, you need something from city hall to prove who you are.'

'But... but... my passport proves who I am. My resident card proves who I am... They're good enough for entering and leaving the country.' I was making the very common error of trying to use logic in the face of Japanese bureaucracy. I sighed heavily. 'OK, I'll go to city hall and see what I can do.'

Thankfully, the local government office was nearby and still open. I explained that I was trying to rent an apartment and the estate agent needed a copy of my family register but, as a foreigner I didn't have one. 'So is there anything you can give me instead?' The meek middle-aged woman behind the counter looked confused.

'You want to see your family register?'

'No. I don't have one because I'm not Japanese. Is there an equivalent paper for a foreign resident?'

This resulted in a look of horrified confusion from the lady. She stammered a few seconds then shot out of her chair and ran to the back of the office. I could see her whispering frantically to a male colleague, who then ran to an older lady. A breathy confabulation ensued, each person seemingly as perplexed as the other. The older woman ran over to me and I explained the situation again. Without a word, she ran back to her workmates in order to debate a further course of action.

Every single non-Japanese resident must register at their local city office, and here in the middle of Tokyo I would guess that there is a proportionately large foreign population compared to most areas. Yet whenever I had any dealings with the local government staff, they always appeared positively stunned at the very notion of a foreign person living in their neighbourhood, as if they'd never encountered anything like it before. The scene of these three office workers flapping around in confusion was sadly familiar. All I could do was sit and wait as they discussed what to do with me.

Finally, the first woman came over again, checked the situation one more time, still barely unable to fathom that I didn't have a family register. She finally said that they could provide a form that states I do *not* have a register. I was willing to accept anything by this stage, so I agreed.

'How do I get this form?' I asked, simply glad to be doing something positive.

'Let me see...' She consulted a manual on her desk. 'We need a copy of your family register.' I was just about to grab her manual and whack her over the head with it, when she managed to rescue herself by quickly adding, 'Oh. In your case...' More frantic searching of the dog-eared volume (just like at the estate agents', no searchable digital files here) until: 'Ah, we just need to see your resident card.'

I handed my card over, delighted that we were getting somewhere at last.

'By the way,' I ventured, 'If I *did* have a family register, what would I need in order to get a copy?'

'Your resident card, of course.'

So, while my resident card was not good enough to use in lieu of a family register, it *was* good enough to get me the form that I would use in lieu of a family register. And if I did have such a register, my resident card would have been needed to get it.

At last I left city hall with a sheet of paper that triumphantly announced that I did not have a different piece of paper, and I ran back to the estate agent. Mr Plump happily accepted this basic and easily forgeable handout, despite the fact he wouldn't accept the very I.D. with which I had obtained this piece of paper, and we were back in business. Or so I thought.

'OK, write your guarantor's name here,' Mr Plump said, pointing to page eight of the contract. I'd forgotten about the guarantor. Basically every apartment owner requires their tenants to submit the name of someone who will bail them out if, for example, the tenant loses his job or simply decides to leave without paying the rent. In nearly every instance, this would be a parent or other relative. For someone in Japan without any other family (again, the guarantor had to be a Japanese person) this was a big problem. I had some decent local friends, but it seemed just too big a favour to ask. The solution was a guarantor company – essentially an insurance broker who I would need to pay in advance. But I had no choice. I agreed to it, and finally we could add up how much all this would cost.

They needed two months' rent in advance, then the equivalent of one month's rent for the estate agent's fee; plus another month's rent as a damage deposit, and another for the guarantor company.

'And key money, naturally.' Something else I'd forgotten about – a bizarre extra cost, essentially a cash gift to the owner of the building in return for giving me the key – to an apartment I had already paid for – and equal to another month's rent. 'And building insurance.' While useful in case of emergency, it was galling to be *forced* to pay for it. 'Oh, and cleaning.'

'But it looked pretty clean… And surely that's something that I should be able to expect – the right to move into a clean place.'

'But you have to pay it,' was the only reason they could offer. Again, I'd made the mistake of trying to use logic, the surest road to madness when dealing with anything bureaucratic in this country.

In total, I had to pay the equivalent of nearly seven months' rent up front, and that was before I started trying to furnish the place. This was definitely the most expensive break-up of my life.

Why Would She Be Here?

It felt strange to leave the old flat. I did a final tour, which should have been pretty fast considering the size of the place (just a bedroom, a bathroom and a kitchen that blended into the living room), but I took my time, examining every wall, every corner, painfully aware that I may not see them again.

Azumi had avoided me as much as possible since discovering the incriminating lipstick on my shirt collar. She asked me to make myself scarce too, so we had each spent most of our time either working, meeting friends, or – in my case – preparing my new apartment. My Japanese skills had been tested to the limit as I called the electric company, the gas company, two water companies, the phone company, and a separate internet provider in order to start their services. There's no more difficult task in a foreign language than speaking to someone over the phone. Without the assistance of gestures, body language, or any supporting materials, relying solely on my ability to *listen* and process every word, and needing to make myself understood through my non-native pronunciation… well, it was nearly as bad as a day at the estate agents'. As well as the emotional wrench of breaking up with my long-term girlfriend, I was realising just how much I had relied upon Azumi to help me navigate my way through life in Japan.

I suppose it was good for me to be more independent again.

When living alone in Tochigi on first arriving in the country, my Japanese had improved dramatically as I simply had to learn words in order to survive. But since moving to Tokyo and living with Azumi, I had all too often been happy to take a backseat in shops and restaurants, conceding that it was quicker and easier to let her take the reins in so many situations. This was due partially to laziness, but also borne out of frustration: in a restaurant, for example, I would order a meal, then clench my buttocks with irritation as the waitress double-checked my request with my Japanese companion. Or, when I ask a question about something on the menu, she would give her answer to the Japanese person at the table. It was all too convenient, then, to slide into the passive role, and my language skills had definitely suffered as a result.

Difficult as it was to rent the new flat, deal with city hall bureaucracy, and call the utility companies, it was good for my confidence to discover that I *could* do these things when I had to.

But all of that seemed irrelevant as I closed the door of the flat I had shared with Azumi the past two years, turned the key in the lock, walked downstairs to the building entrance, and slid my key into our – no, Azumi's – post box.

My new apartment was just five minutes' walk away. I had so many friends in Hirai, and I regarded the area as home, so I had decided to stay nearby. Deep down, too, I still held out hope that perhaps Azumi and I might reconcile in the future.

I stepped inside and noticed how cold it felt, so antiseptic and unlived in. The air was filled with the smell of fresh paint and new furniture, and the walls were white and bare.

For a couple of hours, I felt nothing but despair and loneliness. Then, ever so slowly, a faint pang of excitement developed in my stomach, the thrill of possibility. I was completely liberated, able to do anything, go anywhere. It was a Saturday night, I was a single guy in Tokyo, and I was free to stay out as late as I wanted and go utterly crazy if I wished...

I made a ham toastie, opened a can of beer, and watched *Raiders of the Lost Ark* on my new Blu-Ray player.

I veered between depression and elation for the next few weeks as the school term picked up pace. It's remarkable how quickly situations can change. Whether it be the death of a loved one or a painful break-up, at any moment something can come along that will knock us off course and make even the most routine task feel like an insurmountable obstacle. It seems so unfair that after such an event we are expected to carry on as normal. There were times when I suddenly felt a surge of emotion about to drown me completely, and all I wanted to do was collapse to the floor of the classroom and scream with sadness and frustration. Each time I just managed to stave it off; yet in any of these moments, nobody would congratulate me on my fortitude and professionalism because, as far as they were concerned, it was just another day. Conversely, if I *had* given in to the darkness and allowed myself – just one time – to fall into a minor nervous breakdown, then everyone would have been appalled by my inability to keep my emotions in check.

Thankfully, I had grown used to the routine at school by now, and this helped me get through those tough weeks. Ms Ikuta's classes were still a joy, the students' English skill improving in front of our eyes. Within a few months we had progressed from 'Hello, how are you?' to the stage where the kids could enjoy conversations about last weekend, their future goals, their dreams and fears. I could even roll with Ms Hasebe's annoying habits to a large extent. Ms Maki and I would do our best to wrestle control away from her and help those classes officially under her tutelage. But she still had her moments...

After an especially tedious meeting one Wednesday, all of the teachers went to a nearby *izakaya* to debrief and wind down. It was a surprisingly casual affair, unlike the usual events at upscale French restaurants, and it was a relaxed, enjoyable occasion. Mr Kubo, the ferocious history teacher, once again sang the praises of various Shakespearean actors, then posited his theory that Japan and Britain are essentially mirror images of one another. Each is an archipelago at the far side of a continent and of similar size.

'Britain is in Europe, but not in Europe; Japan is in Asia, but not in Asia. We're different from our neighbours, detached.' He made further comparisons, equating the theatre of Shakespeare and Marlowe with the stylised tradition of *noh* and *kabuki*; he suggested that our respective economies were similarly based on ingenuity rather than natural resources; even our codes of ethics stemmed from the martial traditions of the knight and the samurai. It was a fascinating discussion, but as beer turned to *sake* and my favourite *awamori*, it descended into each of us simply pointing at the other and slurring the phrase, 'Like a mirror… A mirror.'

I thought I had held my drink pretty well – until I overshot my station on the way home and ended up a few stops down the line. Thankfully, it wasn't the last train so I could rectify the situation quickly. Still, it was with a heavy head and delicate stomach that I made my way to school the next morning.

The entire staffroom was under the fog of a collective hangover that morning, but everyone struggled to get through the morning announcements before heading to class. Ms Hasebe's seat at the desk next to me was conspicuously empty, before she scuttled in just after the meeting ended.

'I have to help the Principal with something in the first period,' she told me. 'You can teach the third years without me.'

'Sorry?' I thought I may have misunderstood. I hadn't been scheduled to even be in that class; now she was telling me to teach it solo at a moment's notice. There was no time to argue that I wasn't even legally allowed to teach alone (not having a Japanese teacher's qualification; I was an *assistant* teacher). And my hungover state meant that I didn't have the quick-wittedness to question the situation.

'Should I ask Ms Maki to join me? She's due to help Ms Ikuta, but I'm sure she'd be happy to–'

'No!' At the time I didn't catch the panic in her voice. She regained her composure. 'No, I think she's very busy with the second year classes today.'

172

'Well, alright, but what should I teach? I haven't got anything prepared.'

'Umm…' She grabbed a pile of worksheets from her desk and gave them to me. 'Just have them do these.'

'OK…' I ran upstairs to the classroom, my head spinning. The handouts she had given me would not keep the class occupied for a fifty-minute lesson, but at least they might buy me some time while I thought of another activity.

I entered the room, still flustered, and rushed through the formal greeting with the class leaders. I told them that Ms Hasebe was detained then handed out the worksheet to begin the class. As they passed them around, there was a murmur of confusion.

'Is everything OK?' I asked, sensing that everything was most definitely *not* OK. The murmur turned into laughter as the students showed me their completed homework – exactly the same worksheet that I had just given them.

'Ms Hasebe gave it to us yesterday,' the class leader announced, holding back his mirth and clearly thinking I must have gone mad.

'Oh.' There followed a few improvised activities as I attempted to regain my composure and the students' respect. I'm not sure I achieved either goal, and all the while, I was wondering why the Principal would request a meeting with Hasebe when she had a lesson timetabled. Confusion and anxiety enveloped me, and I was relieved when the Big Ben chimes rang for the end of class.

I was due to teach the next period with Hasebe again so I ran down to the staffroom to find her. She wasn't at her desk, so I knocked on the Principal's office door. He grunted for me to enter and I peeped my head round the door.

'Is Ms Hasebe here?' The Principal gave me a similar look to the one I had received from the students after giving them the worksheet.

'Why would she be here?'

'Oh. Sorry. I just thought… Sorry.' I retreated just as Hasebe entered the staffroom. She was looking red and sweaty. 'Are you alright?' I asked. By this point I was wondering (and possibly hoping) that she'd been fired, or at least rebuked in some way.

'Come on, we'll be late!' We took the elevator up to the language lab on the fifth floor. Thankfully, this was an elective lesson – just ten students swotting up on entrance tests for prospective high schools, and a much easier proposition than being faced with a class of thirty-five kids. As we reached the lab, Hasebe said that she'd be in the adjacent office in order to finish some marking. I was irritated to be forced to teach on my own again, but at least this time my role was more to guide students through practice tests and answer any queries they had.

Halfway through the class, one of the kids was working on an essay and asked me for an English translation of a particular Japanese word. I wasn't familiar with the term, so I said I'd check with Ms Hasebe in the next room.

I knocked on the connecting door and opened it slowly. As I entered, I heard a strange, sudden banging noise – but there was no-one there. 'Hello?' I quickly realised that the noise was coming from the store cupboard. I approached it warily, reached out and turned the handle…

Before I could pull the door open, Hasebe pushed through from the other side. Her hair was sticking up at the side and her left cheek bore the tell-tale red mark of having been rested on a hard surface.

'What is it?' she snapped as she brushed past me and into the office. 'I was just… umm… checking the stationery.' I looked inside the store cupboard. On the linoleum floor, her cardigan was balled up into a pillow, and next to it was her phone. I picked it up and passed it to her. As I did, I saw that she had the timer counting down till ten forty, the end of the lesson period.

It's Complicated

I paced around to keep warm on the chilliest morning of the autumn so far. I was standing in front of Jiyugaoka station, in one of the more affluent districts of western Tokyo. Little bohemian cafes and arty boutiques were opening for the day on either side of me when a sleek blue sports car pulled up at the kerb and the window wound down.

'Long time no see!' the occupant called, and the passenger door swung open. I stooped to get inside under the convertible roof. 'It's good to see you.'

Eri had been a student of mine at the language school in Tochigi a couple of years before. Tall and strikingly beautiful, she was a former nurse who had married the superstar surgeon in her hospital while still in her early twenties. After becoming a housewife, she came to English classes to brush up her language skills (she had previously followed her husband on a short posting in Washington, D.C.), but I think as much as anything else she was simply a little bored as her husband worked long hours at the hospital. She had also told me and her classmates that she suspected her husband's repeated nights away may not always have been job-related. In this regard, it was interesting how frank a lot of students would be with one another when using their second language. In a country where so much is left unsaid, many people seemed to feel less inhibited in

English, and I would often hear them reveal the kind of dark secrets that I very much doubt they would have felt comfortable sharing in Japanese. I know that some Tokyo psychotherapists offer English-language sessions to their patients for the same reason – it just feels easier to spill one's guts in a foreign tongue, the words freed of the weight and stigma attached to many Japanese utterances.

Eri had often specifically requested my lessons, so I was aware that she liked me at some level. This became even more evident when she continued coming to my classes after she and her husband had move to Yokohama, over a hundred kilometres away. Then, when I told the students I would be leaving, she burst into tears, ran to a local shop and bought me a large bouquet of flowers.

I don't even remember telling her the name of my new school in Tokyo, but within days of starting work there, my boss told me that a new student had joined because of me. I was initially a bit concerned when I heard this – *Who could this stalker be?* – so I was relieved and rather pleased when Eri arrived for her first one-to-one lesson. My new school was much closer to her home in Yokohama, and it made more sense for her to join my class there than continue taking a three-hour round trip back to Tochigi every week. And even though I was seeing Azumi at the time, it was still a nice ego boost to have this cheerful, attractive woman choose to come and see me every Thursday morning.

It had been ten months since I had stopped working at that conversation school. In the meantime, Eri and I had exchanged a few texts but hadn't met again until now, zipping through narrow residential streets in her two-seater BMW. She wore a short, body-hugging knit dress and boots that accentuated the toned lines of her legs as they gently pushed the pedals.

'Where are we going for coffee?' I asked.

'I thought we'd go back to mine. It's not far.'

'Oh, right,' I said as nonchalantly as possible, like I did this all the time. 'Is your husband at work?'

'I don't know. We... broke up.'

Thankfully, she had been left with their apartment, a large and tastefully appointed pad on the border of Tokyo and Yokohama. It was on the nineteenth floor, enjoying breathtaking, uninterrupted views of Mt Fuji and the futuristic city skyline.

Eri prepared some coffee and set out plates of homemade cake on the kitchen counter, but we only managed a few bites before we pushed the crockery aside, and we were wrapped in each other's arms. Very soon, the kitchen counter was being used for an entirely different purpose.

'Let's go to the bedroom,' I suggested as we rested, sweaty and entwined on the living room sofa.

'I've got a better idea,' she said, and led me to the bathroom, a huge space with a Jacuzzi, attached steam room, and soft, ambient lighting. Surrounded by wall mirrors reflecting off each other, I couldn't help but think once more, *How the hell did I end up here?*

Despite hitting my early thirties, I still saw myself as a big kid. I had lived in four countries, travelled to thirty more, and experienced so many things, good and bad. I'd been lucky enough to have my fair share of girlfriends over the years, and of course I'd just come out of a serious, cohabiting relationship; yet I always felt like I'd kind of stumbled into all of these situations, while the other people around me – the real grown-ups – led their carefully designed lives with composure and self-assured swagger. *They* were the ones who made love to elegant women in luxurious apartments, not me… But here I was surrounded by about two dozen reflected images of me doing just that with this slender, statuesque beauty.

After a long bath, we dried ourselves and each other (even the towels were a cut above what I was accustomed to – thick, soft and plush). It was beginning to get dark and I suggested we go to bed. I was feeling sleepy after the exercise and warm bath.

'Let's go back to the living room,' Eri said, and I was happy to follow her lead, the lights of central Yokohama sparkling in front of a silhouetted Mt Fuji. We made love yet again, before finally finishing that homemade cake. Then Eri said she'd drive me back to the station.

'Can't I stay over?' I asked.

'Umm… maybe next time,' she said, her eyes flitting away from mine for a moment.

We kissed again then moved to the entrance area. She opened the bedroom door to go and get her coat – and I happened to glance over her shoulder from the corridor. Hanging on the wardrobe door was a man's suit.

'Oh.' I realised instantly that I wasn't supposed to have seen it, but Eri must have clocked my surprise as she came back into the corridor. She opened her mouth to speak, then stopped. She turned crimson and laughed nervously.

'It's…' She struggled for the right words. 'It's complicated.'

I smiled. It was actually something of a relief. Eri was beautiful and sweet, but I didn't see us as a potential long-term couple.

'It's OK,' I said, and she let out a sigh. She looked to the front door, then at her watch.

'Umm, we better get out of here.'

This should probably be the part of the story when I say that I never saw Eri again. Needless to say, only an awful human being would knowingly continue an affair with a married woman. Well, I'm an awful human being.

We never went to her place again – I didn't ask why – but for the next few months, Eri and I regularly met for lunch or coffee, which we would consume hastily before going to the decidedly less salubrious surroundings of my studio flat just under the train tracks. On a couple of occasions, she paid for us to stay at a five-star hotel on the Yokohama waterfront, from where we could actually see her apartment building. I resisted the urge to check if her husband was at home or not, and I prayed that he didn't own a telescope.

The thrilling adult-ness of our relationship was accentuated by Eri's exquisite taste in clothing, especially her lingerie. One of the great disappointments of early adulthood had been the shocking realisation that women do not always have time to pick out identically coloured pants and bra every morning. But with Eri, it was clear that she made a special effort. Her underwear was tastefully expensive, always matching, and usually complemented by pull-up stockings, French knickers or a Basque, which she liked to model mock-coquettishly, allowing me to drink the whole picture in slowly. She was eager to know what I thought of each piece of underwear before allowing me to remove them. Best of all, I never saw the same set of lingerie more than once. It was like making love to a Bond girl.

Stay or Rest?

Believe it or not, during this period I missed Azumi terribly. When we had been together, there was no need to make plans at the weekend; we had each other to hang out with – going to coffee shops, seeing films together, or just staying home and binge watching TV dramas from the UK or US. Of course, we had other things to do and other people to spend time with, but they were exceptions, pleasant interludes.

Now, single, I needed to find ways to fill every free moment; otherwise it was all too easy to sink into a well of regret and loneliness. I had my rugby team, but our games were intermittent. My friends could be relied upon to meet up for beers in the evening, but it was the days that I struggled with. I would go to cafes and read a book or work on my Master's, but I could only drink so many cups of coffee in a day. I felt self-conscious going to the cinema by myself, and staying in my pokey one-room flat simply felt too oppressive. There were entire Saturdays and Sundays when I felt purposeless, almost counting down the hours until the evening, when I could meet up with friends and feel human again.

These nights tended to fall into a pattern. An *izakaya* first, where we would fill up on skewered chicken and vegetables. Then to a British pub or standing bar, before a taxi to Roppongi or Shibuya for the night clubs. I was turning into the archetypal Tokyo *gaijin*, the ones that I had pitied in the past as dull and unadventurous.

At this juncture I know that I'm supposed to realise the error of my ways, the shallowness of such an existence, but these nights out were the best part of my weekend – after getting through all day alone it felt cathartic to drink and talk with friends, and to chat up members of the opposite sex. For all my genuine sadness about Azumi, it was also novel and exciting to know that I could flirt with various women in good conscience. I no longer had to hold back, telling myself that what I had with Azumi was worth more than a one-night stand, because – well – I was no longer with her.

A few of these encounters were one-offs, nights of mad, drunken lust not to be repeated, but I also arranged to catch up with some of these women again. My confidence beginning to soar, I felt more relaxed meeting people in other situations too – in coffee shops or even on the train platform – and before long I had cultivated a small circle of female companions. These were not girlfriends as such, but women I could meet on weeknights too, for dinner, drinks, and – at times – love hotels. I've mentioned previously how a lot of young people in Japan stay with their parents until getting married. This is partly due to tradition, like so many things in the country, but also as a way to avoid paying the high rents and extortionate signing-on fees that apartments command. Naturally, this situation created a need for places where young lovers could meet in private, hence the proliferation of these love hotels – about thirty thousand spread across the nation – with rooms that couples could rent by the night or by the hour, and specifically designed for sex.

I had first made use of them with Azumi, back when I lived in Tochigi and she was lodging with her family in Tokyo. Rather than sleeping on their living room floor – with nothing but a sliding paper door between us and her sleeping mother (at least I hope she was sleeping), and where we would be woken in the morning by her four-year-old nephew jumping on top of us – we could stay cheaply and in relative comfort at a love hotel.

Famously, some of these establishments are built in the shape of gaudy cruise ships or Cinderella castles, but those are usually in the suburbs, where real estate is more freely available. In central Tokyo, love hotels are usually more conventional box-shaped buildings with odd faux-English names like Hotel Joy Plus, Hotel Neverland, or – worryingly – Hotel Kid. The entrances are discreetly shrouded in curtains, allowing a swift entrance under the drapes. In the reception area, couples can look at pictures of the available rooms. These are often fairly basic places that would not look out of place in a standard business motel, while others are garish shrines to Japan's decadent 'Bubble Era' of the eighties and nineties – all brass fittings, disco balls and mirrored ceilings.

After selecting a room with the push of a button, the couple goes to the front desk, where the receptionist sits behind a small, low window, unable to see the customers' faces. It is usually an older lady, for some reason, and she asks the standard question, 'Stay or rest?' Then she takes the money and slides a key over the counter for the lovers to make their own way to the room.

One of the more awkward experiences was when my

companion and I would end up sharing the cramped lift with another couple. There was always a lot of throat clearing and staring at the elevator ceiling, and a veritable sense of relief as soon as one pair had alighted.

This being Japan, the rooms are always spotless and well-appointed with fresh towels, robes and toiletries. There is a whole cottage industry in love hotel cleaning services, and it was not uncommon to spot a truck at the back of the building, picking up dirty mattresses and blankets and exchanging them for fresh ones. That's right – between each visit, they strip not just the sheets but the entire bed before the next couple enters, making the whole experience marginally less icky.

As well as a king-sized bed, a sofa and a massive TV, there is a large en suite bathroom with Jacuzzi capability and multi-coloured lighting, as well as a waterproofed TV and, occasionally, an inflatable sun lounger, in case the couple wishes to lie down under the shower or indulge in an oil massage.

Back in the main room, the bed always has a panel of buttons and dials in the headboard, from which we can control the numerous lights, music and air-conditioning, and sometimes make the bed vibrate or even rotate. There are often microphones too, just in case the lovers feel like a spot of karaoke, and games consoles for a quick round of *FIFA* if so desired, but I never made use of these, I'm happy to say.

The worst of the initial post-breakup loneliness was wearing off now, and as well as the crazy weekend nights, I began to fill the days too, meeting Yuki, Mai, Chihiro or Reiko for afternoon coffee or a walk in the park – before heading to my place or hers, or enjoying a daytime 'rest' in Hotel Yes One, where each room was themed after a particular city – the New York suite was chrome and black leather, Barcelona was all Gaudi-esque curves, while Stockholm was filled with Ikea furniture, therefore almost identical to my own hastily furnished flat.

I continued seeing Eri, the doctor's wife, as well, and at times my life had a touch of the screwball farce about it as I rushed from one date to another. On one occasion, Yuki, a dauphin-esque yoga instructor, found a contact lens on the edge of my bathroom sink. It belonged to Sayaka, the nursing student who had stayed over the night before. Taken off guard, I blurted out that it was mine. From then on I had to pretend that I wore contacts every time I met Yuki, which became even trickier when she asked for my advice on a good brand.

I'm sure that some readers are now thinking that I'm a terrible person, and that is of course their prerogative. I've no doubt that my existence looked shallow and unfulfilling to some outsiders. However, each of these relationships was in itself warm and respectful, and I was always careful to make it clear that I was recently out of a serious relationship so not ready to commit to anything long-term. With each of my new friends, we enjoyed each other's company and shared some lovely memories. The fact that we also had sex did not negate any of that; rather it complemented and enhanced the experience and, as far as I'm aware, we all enjoyed ourselves immensely. So there.

I've Had Enough of This

'We've noticed you usually leave at four o'clock. Is everything alright?' Mr Arakawa, the kindly Vice-Principal, seemed genuinely concerned.

'Umm, yes,' I replied, feeling a pang of foreboding. 'That's when I'm supposed to leave, isn't it?'

'We spoke to your dispatch company. They said you should stay till five.'

'Oh. That's... interesting. I'm pretty sure my contract says I should leave at four...'

The JET (Japan Exchange and Teaching) programme was established by the government in the nineteen-seventies to encourage increased cultural exchange between Japan and people from overseas. Primarily, it worked to bring Assistant Language Teachers (ALTs) into school classrooms in order to improve students' international awareness and language skills, while giving foreign university graduates a taste of Japanese life.

The programme grew steadily until its peak in the mid-nineties when it had nearly seven thousand participants at any given time, and by all accounts it served all parties well – salaries were comparatively good (especially during Japan's economic 'Bubble Era') and this meant that competition was high, allowing the Education Boards to be selective in who they employed. Sadly, a restructuring at the turn of the century led to a steady reduction in the number of JET participants. Local education authorities, suddenly deprived of foreign ALTs at a time when the Education Ministry was insisting that English classes be expanded, needed to look elsewhere. And this led to the rise of the private ALT dispatch companies. Much like any temporary employment agency, they offered to take the strain of finding and training new employees – in return for a fee – and they would hire teachers from inside and outside Japan, who would then be assigned to schools around the country.

The agency that employed me was the biggest in the country, but they hadn't covered themselves in glory when they had misinformed me that I was going for a *senior* rather than *junior* high school position before my interview with the Board of Education. Since then, however, I'd had very few dealings with them other than a minor dispute when they hadn't paid my transport costs as promised in my first couple of months. This was 'an accidental oversight' that I was to later learn seemed to happen to everyone who ever worked for them. Very few teachers (many of whom were new in Japan) ever complained, so the company probably made a small fortune from this unfortunate 'oversight'.

When the Vice-Principal asked about my working hours, I was naturally concerned, so I sent an email to my local supervisor, Lee, to ask for clarification. It was polite and measured as, at this stage, I had no reason to believe it was anything other than a simple misunderstanding.

A couple of hours later, I checked my inbox to find a reply from Lee. The tone was friendly enough and he asked me to come and see him at the agency's central office, 'Whenever you have time.' He had copied in one of his colleagues, Jason, but clearly didn't realise that he'd also included an earlier mail that he had sent to Jason after receiving my initial query. It read:

Another whiner. I'll deal with him.

I was offended by the label of 'whiner', of course. More importantly, the message made me suspect that there was more going on than an innocent mistake. Clearly, this was not a one-off incident.

I replied to tell him that I didn't appreciate his unprofessional manner, especially after a perfectly polite and legitimate question. Rather than apologise, Lee went on the offensive, saying that I had breached the terms of my contract by discussing that contract with the school. This was kind of genius – my school was being given incorrect information about my working conditions by the agency; but if I tried to rectify the discrepancy because it was against my terms of employment, I was then supposedly breaking those terms.

Lee instructed me to come to the head office the following day. I agreed to do this, but only during my contracted work hours. This was partly out of a sense of fair play – why should I give up my free time for them? – but also because I knew that the agency would then have to tell my school I was unavailable to teach while I had the meeting. It was important to me that the Vice-Principal and the Board of Education knew what was going on.

So the next afternoon, I arrived in Iidabashi, one of my favourite parts of Tokyo, full of cobbled streets and traditional Japanese craft shops, but with a distinct European twist in its abundance of French and Spanish restaurants. Unfortunately, rather than sipping espresso on the waterside terrace of Canal Café, or watching a double bill at the local repertory cinema, I was trudging toward the dispatch company's office with an expanding knot of anxiety in my stomach.

I hate confrontation of any kind. I'm the type of person who receives an undercooked dish at a restaurant and simply eats around the pink bits rather than cause a scene by sending it back. So it was with growing dread that I entered the building. My confidence in the company was not increased by its décor. Nothing looked permanent – just very simple desks with nothing on them, no pictures on the walls or signage of any kind, and very few staff. Despite being the largest company of its kind in Japan, their office gave the impression that they were ready to pack up and move out overnight should things go awry.

Lee was a shaven-headed, muscle-bound Texan with small, black, intense eyes. He came and met me at the front desk (there was no receptionist) and led me through to a small side office with three plastic chairs and office-standard grey carpet. He moved one seat into the corner of the room and offered it to me. I sat down, already feeling my face going red as it tends to do in any fight-or-flight situation. He then moved the other two chairs directly in front of me and sat down in one of them. He didn't say anything, just sighed and

191

tapped his foot impatiently.

I blathered something about the weather, but he wasn't interested. He was looking to the door, waiting, and a moment later, Jason entered. Another imposing figure, he was an Australian with a patchy black beard and slicked-back hair. He took the other chair and shifted it closer to me so that I had to recoil just to prevent our knees from touching. The three of us were in a tight triangle, me with my back to the wall, physically trapped, literally cornered.

I had been so worried that I would crack under pressure, so I had written a note on my hand to help me remember what I wanted to say, but now it was blurring in my sweat. However, just knowing it was there was reminder enough. I sensed that they would try to lead me off the track or get me flustered with redundant points, so I had written:

Contract, 4pm

Labour Laws

I told myself to stick to these points, having researched the laws (which the government had helpfully translated into English on their website) the night before. Basically, the company couldn't make me work any hours outside my contract, and if they *did* expect me to work later, not only would they have to pay me overtime, but I would also be working more than thirty hours a week, thus changing my official status from part-time to full-time and entitling me to health insurance, pension payments and other benefits that all full-timers must receive. I even brought a printout of these laws with the important points highlighted.

I repeated the contents of the note in my mind like a mantra. Lee and Jason edged their seats even closer in a blatant attempt to physically intimidate me. It was working. I was shaking, sweaty, breathing too fast.

Lee started by shouting at me for discussing my contract with the Vice-Principal, pointing his finger in my face. I tried not to look at him; I kept my eyes on the floor and replied that I simply stated my finish time – something that the school had a right to know. Jason, trying to be the good cop at this stage, explained in patronising tones about Japanese workers often working late. 'It's part of the culture here.'

I responded that the people who did this were usually full-time staff, and my contract was officially part-time; besides which, I could only base my position on the Japanese labour laws, not on perceived cultural norms. 'I've got a copy of it here.'

At the sight of the labour laws, there was a change in atmosphere, a little more conciliatory. The smoothness at the way they worked together told me that they had dealt with these situations before, but I guessed that they were usually browbeating a new arrival in the country who could easily be hoodwinked or cajoled into towing the company line. They looked surprised by this move and changed tack. Jason started talking about their manager, a sweet older man who was apparently losing weight through stress. 'He's doing all he can to keep these contracts with the Education Boards. If we lose another one... well, I worry about him.'

When I didn't change my stance, Lee tried another approach:

'We just had a hundred new teachers in training last month. I'm sure that they would all love to work in a school like yours.' I nearly laughed at the transparency of his threat, but my gums were too dry to form a smile properly. I was less amused when Jason added: 'Our reports from your school about you haven't been great. I'm sure they won't mind if a different ALT joins them next year.' This really stung. Despite my early misgivings, especially with Ms Hasebe, I felt that I was appreciated by the other teachers. It was disappointing to hear otherwise. Still, I didn't take the bait. I just sighed and tried to stay cool, even as I felt tears begin to form.

God, I'm pathetic.

As mentioned previously, I am terrible at arguing, but my resolution to stick to my notes had inadvertently turned me into a tougher opponent than I had anticipated. Whether they were trying to scare me, guilt me, or pretend that we were all mates in the same boat ('We all know how it is; sometimes we have to help each other out a bit'), I simply stayed with what I'd summarised in the now illegible scribble on my hand: 'I don't know anything about that, but I do know that my contract states I work till four p.m., and I also know that Japanese labour laws say that if you want me to work longer than thirty hours a week, then I should be treated as a full-time worker.'

As much as I'd like to think that I was cool as a cucumber, deflecting their attacks with wit and pithy comebacks, I was actually sweating like a pig, and my face must have been either puce-coloured or deathly white. I just made sure that my voice stayed level and calm, even when they raised theirs, and I stuck to my notes. Before long, I realised an amazing thing – I was winning. They didn't know how to argue against me. I wasn't talking myself into corners, I wasn't trying to outshout them or push back against their bullying tactics, and I wasn't compromising at all. When I needed time to think, I took as long as I needed, and I didn't let them rush me into blurting out something I would regret later. When I felt my throat become too dry to say something, I didn't try to force out a nervous squeak; again, I remained quiet. I thought this was weakness on my part, but it turned out to be my greatest strength – just staying silent. I realised that they were trying to get some kind of response from me, but when I said nothing, they ended up trying to fill that silence and invariably said something that contravened the labour laws – which I had in front of me!

After half an hour, they just seemed to run out of arguments. Lee suddenly said, 'I've had enough of this,' and got up. Jason followed and I could finally take a gulp of air.

'See you at next week's meeting,' was all Jason said as he exited. It appeared that I was free to go.

Career Suicide

The next morning, as the routine staff meeting came to a close, the Vice-Principal Mr Arakawa said, 'Garett, please come to the Principal's office.'

Bloody hell, I thought. This was getting a bit scary. Ever since my very first day when the Principal had shouted at me about the old ALT who brought a toy snake to school, I had done all I could to avoid him. While he seemed to have softened towards me over time, he still had a suspicious glare in his eye whenever he looked at me.

I entered his room with Mr Arakawa beside me. We sat down on the low easy chairs that were weirdly difficult to perch on while remaining businesslike. Ms Ikuta joined us, then the Principal sat next to me. I genuinely had no clue which way this was going.

The Principal had a faxed document (the Japanese love their faxes) in his hand, which he laid out on the table. Ms Ikuta translated as the Principal spoke:

'This is the contract between the Board of Education and the dispatch agency...'

Yikes, I mouthed. This was becoming more and more serious. The Principal went on to explain the details, including the working hours for the ALT – *eight till five*. My first reaction was a sigh of defeat. This appeared to back up the dispatch company's line of argument against me, and it would be very hard to refute it without showing my contract – which I legally wasn't allowed to do. And Jason had told me the day before that the school had given me a poor performance report, so clearly no-one would mind if this spelled the end of my tenure.

Before I had time to think of my next course of action, the Principal added something else, which I didn't understand. He smiled, for the first time ever in my presence. I looked to Ms Ikuta.

'The Principal says that he asked the Board of Education to find out why there's a difference between this contract and what they tell you. He says they should be paying you more if they expect you to work later.'

I was quite stunned by this. The Principal had no reason to stick his neck out for me, especially as I had thought he saw me as nothing more a necessary nuisance. But now he was taking my side against the dispatch company, and enlisting the local government's help too!

'But… they told me that my report from the school was bad.' I really had been hurt by Jason's revelation the previous day. In fact, of everything that had happened in the company head office, this was the one detail that I kept replaying in my mind. I was truly upset by it. Ms Ikuta looked surprised when she heard this, but she dutifully translated into Japanese. There followed a brief discussion between the Principal, Mr Arakawa and Ms Ikuta before the Vice-Principal left the room.

'Just a moment,' Ms Ikuta said, and within seconds the Mr Arakawa returned with a piece of paper and placed it on the table in front of me. It was the evaluation report about my performance in the school that had been sent to the Education Board and my agency: the Principal had given me top scores in nearly every category.

I was blown away, incredibly moved after the tension of the previous few days and the genuine fear that I was not wanted and might lose my job. The school was on my side! Clocking my surprise, he smiled again and turned to English: 'You, Garett. Stay at this school.'

I was still speechless as I left the office alongside Ms Ikuta. 'You'd better tell the other ALTs in the area – they might want to talk to their schools too.'

This was good thinking. It was one thing having a single school support their ALT in a dispute of this kind, but if I could get the other ALTs and other schools on board, then we could make real changes – perhaps even be treated as genuine full-time workers and receive insurance and all the other benefits. I had a free period, so I immediately sent out an email to the other ALTs explaining the situation – that the company was trying to deceive us and the schools by making us work full-time hours for part-time wages. I suggested that each ALT talked to their respective schools to clarify working times. I also recommended a quick conference before our scheduled meeting with Jason the following week – a chance to clarify our collective position.

By lunchtime I had responses from all the ALTs, supporting my stance and agreeing to the idea of a meeting. Things were happening.

The only colleague less than vociferous in his approval was Graeme, the sole ALT in the area who had been in his role the previous year. By chance, I bumped into him on my commute home that evening. While trying to avoid inhaling his peculiarly smelly breath, I listened to him tell me in his infuriating *I-know-everything* tone that the Board of Education was too closely linked to the dispatch company and would never support us. When I disagreed and gave more detail about the way my school's Principal had taken my side, he smiled condescendingly: 'Oh, he would say that; they always do. But they'll never support us.'

'Will you at least stand alongside us if all the ALTs ask the company to explain their action?'

This put him in a tough spot. He saw himself as a bastion of liberal ideals (ironically for someone who seemed to hate nearly every race of people), so he could hardly be seen to go against collective action. 'OK,' he finally agreed. 'But we're committing career suicide.'

Jason was due to meet us at Jim's school the next Wednesday afternoon, so the four ALTs for junior high schools in the area – Jim, Graeme, Rob and myself – all met at lunchtime in the conference room (which, incidentally, had a fully stocked liquor cabinet and a fridge full of bottled beer). We all agreed that we had to show a united front and let Jason know that if the dispatch company wanted us to work longer hours, then we expected full-time pay and conditions. Even Graeme seemed more on board now, suggesting that 'As the longest serving ALT, maybe I should speak first.' I have to admit that I felt a bit peeved by this. It was as if he was now trying to paint himself as the architect of any improvement in our working conditions, when it had been me who had instigated this and risked everything in the first place. However, I soon realised that I was being petty, and instead I should be pleased that everyone was ready to fight together. I agreed that he could speak first.

When Jason arrived, he began by reminding us that he had a degree in Management (as he had done at all previous meetings), then re-ran his argument from the week before – that in Japanese culture people were often expected to work more than was stated in their contracts. He also repeated his barely veiled threat that new arrivals were joining the company every week, and they would all be delighted to work in our area.

We sat quietly and listened. This was fine, I thought. Much like my solo encounter the week before, we would just let him wear himself out, then reply with our demands of full-time pay and benefits in return for full-time hours. Jason finished by saying that as all the ALTs were relatively new, then it wouldn't be good for anyone to rock the boat with the Education Board. At last, Jason sat down, apparently pleased with his speech. There was a moment's quiet, in which I looked to Graeme. He had asked to represent our position first, but he wasn't doing anything.

'Graeme?' I prompted, and he seemed to wake from his reverie. He smiled at Jason, then at his three fellow ALTs. It was a look of absolute confidence, as if to say *Don't worry, guys, I've got this.*

'Thank you for coming here today, Jason,' he began. 'We all really appreciate it.' I thought this was a bit toadying, but I accepted it as Graeme's strategy for buttering up his opponent before hitting him with our demands. 'I realise how hard your job must be, and as the longest serving ALT, I know that we are very lucky to be in our schools.'

Come on, mate, get to the point…

'Some people here…' Graeme looked at me. 'Some people here have less experience of working in Japan, and they don't understand how the system works.'

Any second now, surely…

'But don't worry. I've explained to everyone, and I think we're all agreed that things are pretty good as they are.'

What the hell? I realised now that this was no preamble; this was Graeme's main point – to comply with the dispatch company's demands, to work full-time hours without the pay or benefits to match.

Graeme gave his smug smile and looked around at all of us. Everyone was staying quiet, everyone was caving in. Jason stood up again, triumphant.

'Well, I'm glad-'

'Wait a minute!' I interrupted.

Jason sighed and rolled his eyes. 'What now?'

'Graeme isn't speaking for all of us.' I looked to Graeme, who rolled his eyes. 'Sorry, but you're not.' I hated this situation – having to argue against Jason was bad enough, but now I was up

201

against someone else, a colleague who I would have to face a lot more often in future. 'I've spoken to my school, and they agree with me that something's not right. There's been some...' I struggled for the right words. Clearly the dispatch company – Jason included – had lied about our working hours and about my school's evaluation of my performance. But I knew that a direct accusation would just rile Jason even further. 'There's been some... discrepancy. Everyone here works hard at their school, but, like I said last week, if you want us to work full-time hours then we should get full-time conditions. Right, Jim? Rob?'

There was silence. Jim pretended to check some notes, while Rob shuffled uncomfortably in his chair.

You cowardly bastards, I thought. All three of my peers had professed their support for my position beforehand, but in the heat of the argument they had left me to hang. Not only had they passed up on the chance of making positive changes to our working conditions, but they had done it fully aware that by currying favour with the management, my own job was now looking even more precarious. I wouldn't have minded so much if they were fresh faced new recruits just off the plane, but all of them were old enough to know better, and all of them had spent a few years in Japan. Yet they gave up the instant Jason put up any kind of fight. In fact, at this point, Jason was the only person in the room I had any semblance of respect for – at least he had stuck to his guns. But that didn't last long as he grinned at me and said, 'Right, what's next on the agenda?'

A Beautiful Heart

The Culture Festival is a major part of any Japanese school calendar. Much like the run-up to Sports Day in June, the students spent weeks planning and performing various activities each afternoon after school. Then, in the days immediately preceding the event, regular lessons ceased altogether as final preparations were completed. There were exhibitions of paintings, calligraphy and sculpture, and science experiments and mathematics projects were displayed on desks. Mr Kubo, the Anglophile history teacher, directed a stage adaptation of Dickens' *A Christmas Carol*, which would have made a little more sense had this not been early October. The brass band rehearsed even longer than usual, and every class in school practised daily for the choral competition.

I have often heard criticism that the Japanese education system favours rote learning and repetitive practice at the expense of developing creativity, and my own experience bore this out. The Japanese language classes (equivalent, of course, to an English class in a school in the UK) were focused almost entirely on *kanji* drills, as students struggled to repeat and remember the complex pen strokes, in the correct order, of increasingly obscure Chinese characters (students needed to know how to read and write *two thousand* of these by the end of their secondary school education). This left only a little class time for reading classic literature, with no space at all for any creative writing of the children's own. Some of my happiest school memories were of composing stories or expressing my thoughts and opinions through personal essays, but most Japanese students had no experience of this. It genuinely perplexed me how Japan was able to produce any writers or dramatists – and partly explained the paucity of interesting storylines in their television programmes.

Art classes were a little more freeform, and the teacher, Ms Suzuki, was a delightful whirlwind of enthusiasm whom the kids adored. However, it was interesting to see how almost all representations of people were drawn with the cowlick hair and doe eyes so prevalent in manga and anime. There was little development of any individual artistic style, and I struggled to distinguish between different students' artwork. There is surely a fascinating Sociology dissertation to be written by someone more intelligent than me on this phenomenon – even when students were encouraged to be unique, they preferred to copy and perfect an existing style, rather than try something new.

This lack of creative fluidity may go some way to explaining the relative dearth of innovation in all fields – the number of Japanese Nobel Prize winners, for instance, is tiny given the size of the nation's population and wealth. Similarly, it is possible to test the low level of independent thought simply by asking for a burger at McDonald's *with no dressing*, then watch the staff struggle to compute how such a far-out request might be met.

On the other hand, this culture of practising a skill until it is perfect has led to some of the world's leading electronics companies being able to take ideas like the computer or Blu-ray player and make the most reliable versions of them. And, after the initial confusion has dissipated, that McDonald's burger will be freshly cooked, neatly presented, and packaged beautifully.

So, while the Culture Festival was not a feast of new ideas, I was hugely impressed by what I saw. The overall level of art on display was of an excellent standard, as was the science exhibition. Woodwork students constructed colourful sets for Mr Kubo's stage play, and the sewing club made beautiful costumes. The Japanese culture club put together a stunning display of kimono and ikebana, while the art club painted massive banners that would welcome parents and guests to the festival.

As for English, all of the classes displayed their summer homework – an illustrated diary – on the walls of an 'English Corridor' and I was pleased with the end result as the students' hard work flanked visitors on both sides. The problem was that, once the diaries were completed and taped to the walls, I had nothing much to do. Just like Sports Day, I felt redundant and listless, just wandering around and trying to find chores to occupy me. I chatted to students and occasionally helped them with English words on their banners, I pitched in with some heavy lifting as the kids dragged the theatre sets into place onstage, and I even took the time to redecorate the language laboratory with posters and pamphlets that I had procured from various Tokyo embassies (Tanzania was especially generous).

The school had a small English club, which consisted of five very quiet girls who weren't especially keen on the language – but were even less keen on any of the other clubs. To be honest, our twice-weekly meetings could be rather painful as the students would sit silently, waiting for me to entertain them. Coming at the end of the school day, I was usually running low on energy and I had increasing difficulty generating new ways to encourage them to speak. When, just a few days beforehand, Ms Ikuta asked if we could make something for the Culture Festival, my heart sank. The girls were not especially artistic, nor were they confident enough to perform a skit or song. I asked them if they had anything that they would like to do, and I received the usual polite smiles and barely perceptible shrugs. Then Karin, the most responsive of the group, piped up: 'Newspaper.'

It was wonderful to see how enthusiastic the girls became now that they had a clear project to work on, and it shamed me that I hadn't been able to elicit this kind of response before. Within a few minutes, we had brainstormed ideas on what form the paper would take – a four-page A3 handout – then each member volunteered for a role: editors for the school, national and international news sections, plus a features editor (making a quiz and teacher profiles), then an overall editor who would try and put it all together on PC. Twenty-four hours later, the first edition of the *Tokyo Times* came off the press.

It was intended to be a one-off for the Festival, but the *Tokyo Times* became a biweekly publication and the central focus of the English club. I now looked forward to our meetings, and the students clearly enjoyed it too. Through this experience, as well as watching the students become so involved in the Sports Day and Culture Festival, I learned just how motivating projects could be, and this knowledge really helped my teaching in regular classes too. Once there was a final goal – and especially if the work was intended for public display – students would do all they could to produce something good. Like that perfectly packaged McDonald's hamburger, there was real pride in the end product.

The Culture Festival went off without a hitch. I particularly enjoyed *A Christmas Carol*, with the students' acting ability outstripping anything I could find on TV. The chorus competition, too, was impressive, featuring surprisingly complex blends and harmonies, even if the songs themselves – composed and collated in school textbooks especially for these kinds of events – were invariably dull. Again, I wondered why this level of singing skill could not be replicated by the professionals, with Japanese pop music just as bad as its TV (the same agencies wielded all the power in both fields, causing similarly horrible results).

Once the Festival was completed, there was a celebration dinner with the PTA in a nearby swanky hotel. Teachers were each assigned a table at which we were expected to chat to the parents (mostly mothers). Thankfully, my group was an exuberant, slightly flirty bunch who were happy to put up with my patchy Japanese in return for the chance to practise their varying levels of English.

As is usual, the party began with a lot of platitude-filled

speeches. As I've mentioned before, even the shyest Japanese person will become the most interminable windbag once they have a microphone in their hands. This may be acceptable if we are already drinking and enjoying the food, but the pre-toast speech is the scourge of any formal party. It is considered extremely bad form for anybody to take even the smallest sip of drink before the opening toast. However, these toasts are so agonisingly long that you could die of thirst before it's done. There can be great comic value in watching a hundred or more people holding their beer just in front of their parched lips, anticipating the long-awaited Japanese word for 'Cheers' – '*Kanpai*' – the signal to start drinking. Then the speaker (almost always an old man) stumbles upon a new line of thought and the group rolls its collective eyes and licks its lips some more.

At last, the Principal finished his instantly forgettable monologue, we could clink glasses, relax and drink. Another feature of this kind of official party is that the beer comes in batches of one-litre bottles, usually placed within easy reach at the centre of the table. Courtesy dictates that we don't pour our own drinks; instead we serve our neighbours and wait for them to reciprocate. The glasses were small shot-size receptacles so even after one or two sips, someone would usually lean over to give me a refill, and after half an hour it was impossible to judge if I'd drunk half a pint or five bottles' worth. Thankfully, everyone was equally inebriated and I enjoyed getting to know the parents better. I was able to say fairly nice things about all the relevant offspring – my stock phrase about the worst behaved students was 'He's very… active' – and it felt good to feel accepted as part of the wider school community.

To my right was an especially friendly woman who was eager to hear my views about her daughter. Mami chan was a third year student, confident in English and always happy to chat to me after class. With her mum being so friendly, and the effects of beer really kicking in, I felt the need to be especially fulsome in my praise. One of Mami's many good points was her patience with less able classmates. She would often guide them through activities or whisper help when they needed it, and I wanted to share my admiration of this with her mother. When drinking, my Japanese fluency tended to increase; conversely, my memory of vocabulary decreased. So, as I tried to say 'Mami has a really big heart,' I suddenly went blank on the word 'heart.'

Heart... Heart... Got it! It's 'mune'.

I started again: '*Musume wa totemo okii mune aru.*' 'Your daughter has a very big heart.'

Mami's mother looked confused. The other parents at the table stopped chatting and looked at me quizzically. I repeated, slower and louder this time: '*Musume no mune wa totemo okii.*' Just to be clear, I pointed at my chest then stretched out my arms to mime just how big Mami chan's heart was. There was quiet, then a few embarrassed giggles. Something was definitely wrong...

Then it hit me that 'big heart' may have been too idiomatic and didn't translate well into Japanese, so I tried another tack: 'She has a beautiful heart, a great heart... A really pure heart' – '*Kanojyo wa kirei na mune aru, subarashii mune... Totemo pyua na mune.*'

209

This didn't appear to be helping. Mrs Yamada, the very friendly mother of a decidedly unfriendly boy, tried to help me out.

'*Mune?*'

'*Hai, mune...* Heart.'

Everyone at the table burst into laughter, but when I asked why, they all seemed too embarrassed to explain. I checked the dictionary on my phone. *Mune*, in certain contexts, could be used as a synonym of heart. However, its base meaning was a little different.

As I replayed my comments in my head, I felt myself descending into a deep well of shame. Clearly they all saw the funny side, and even Mami's mother was chuckling and punching my arm playfully, but I was bright red and desperate to get out of there.

For once, I avoided the second party and caught an early train home, periodically banging my head against the glass of the sliding door.

Mune meant 'Breasts.'

'Your daughter has really big breasts,' I had told the fifteen-year-old girl's mother, while miming just how extraordinarily massive they were. 'She has beautiful breasts, great breasts... Really pure breasts.'

It Looks Really Bad

The upside to my swift departure after the PTA dinner was that I arrived home before eleven and was able to get an early night. Unfortunately, I didn't sleep well. My 'breasts' comment kept appearing in my dreams then jolting me awake. And then – as I had for the past couple of months now – I would start thinking about my life, about whether I should stay in Japan or consider returning home, about my future goals, and about my family. Most of all, during these regular sleepless nights, I would think about Azumi. How was she? Had she met anyone new? And was there any chance for us to get back together?

I woke from my short sleep with an unfamiliar sensation for a Sunday morning: I didn't have a hangover. This was especially pertinent as I had a big rugby match later that day – the Cup Final, no less.

I had been recruited for the team six months previously, after I got chatting to the captain Kohei, a fast-talking estate agent, at a local *izakaya*. He invited me to practice, and before long I was the team's regular right winger.

I hadn't played much rugby since school, but I had joined a club up in Tochigi, and before my first game there I had made the rather snobbish assumption that I would find it easy – *What do the Japanese know about rugby?* I soon found out, as I struggled to match the technique and fitness of my teammates. Having seen kids in my school practising for various sports clubs, I now knew why. Much like almost every other skill – be it writing *kanji* or learning a choral harmony – your average Japanese kid seemed to have no problem with repeating a training drill over and over again. This made my teammates and opponents experts with the ball, their passing and handling ability far outstripping anything I had come across back home. However, after my initial shock had subsided, I learned that what I lacked in ball mastery I made up for with competitive nous. While many schools had rugby clubs that met for practice every single day, they played very few competitive matches, at least until the students' late teens. So aspects of the game such as positioning at kick-offs and scrums, or knowing when to kick and when to run, were relatively alien concepts. And so I became an unspectacular but surprisingly effective member of the team.

The sports ground, like so many in the city, was directly next to a river. I guess that with space at a premium, these spots were the least likely to be earmarked for development, but it meant that the pitch was repeatedly waterlogged, any loose ball would float out into Tokyo Bay, and the swarms of mosquitoes in summertime were harder to handle than the trickiest opponent. Thankfully, on a still, dry autumn day like this one, the ground was playable, and the only insects were a few crickets in the long grass that separated the touchline from the water.

While the weather was perfect for rugby, our performance just didn't live up to the occasion. We were up against a side that we had beaten easily in the League, yet for all our dominance, we just couldn't turn it into points. As the main kicker, I was especially profligate in front of goal, managing to hit the ball against the bar, the upright, the opposing centre's outstretched hand... pretty much anywhere except between the posts.

The only positive was that we had almost all of the possession, so surely the points would come if we kept our heads and remained patient. Then the opposition centre hoofed a clearance up field, our full back hesitated, and their scrum half scooped up the loose ball and raced over the line for the first points of the game.

We had ten minutes to respond, and our efforts became ever more desperate. We ran and ran, but nothing worked. Then Kohei kicked a long ball in front of me. It was bouncing wildly on the hard, dry surface, but if I could just reach it before their full back...

Their winger was hot on my heels, while the full back charged toward me. It was too far ahead to catch, but I stretched my left leg out, hoping to nudge the ball nearer the try line with my toe. I wasn't looking at the full back, who was leaping in an attempt to get there first, his foot at waist height...

For a few seconds, I blacked out. It was only later that my teammates pieced together for me exactly what had happened: The full back and I were running at top speed toward each other, the ball between us. As I had stretched, so had he – a karate-style flying kick. At the very apex of this kick, the studs of his boot had planted themselves in my crotch, the combined weight of both his jump and mine compounding the impact. Then the winger who was chasing me crashed into my back, exacerbating the force of our collision even further.

I crumpled on the ground, not caring that my tongue was in the mud and clumps of dirt were filling my mouth. All I could feel, all I could think about, was my groin. I could barely breathe – just short, snatched gulps of air. I couldn't speak; instead, I emitted a weird silent scream. I rolled onto my side – *still agony* – then onto my back – *even worse.*

Then the adrenalin kicked in – *We're five points down in the Cup Final. I'm just a bit winded. I'll be fine...*

My teammates pulled me onto my feet. I shuffled gingerly off the pitch and splashed ice cold water onto my crotch. I stretched a bit and told myself I could run it off – we'd used all our replacements and we were down to fourteen men. I signalled to the referee and re-entered the game, prepared to be a hero.

Five minutes later, as every movement sent shocks of agony from my groin through my entire body, I knew I couldn't continue. I cupped my testicles in my hand, and I appeared to be missing one. Conversely, there was a ball-shaped lump in my lower abdomen. This wasn't good. I dragged myself off the pitch again and assumed the foetal position.

We lost the match.

Kohei drove me to the local hospital but, this being a Sunday, it was closed. The next one too. On our third attempt, we found a small clinic that was open, but the septuagenarian doctor just chuckled at my plight and, after a brief inspection, said he couldn't do anything to help. I would have to go to a larger hospital for a specialist to treat me.

An unexpected advantage of living abroad is that you gain a different perspective on the good and bad points of your own country. Seeing the way that public transport ran on time in Japan, or witnessing customers leave their wallets unattended on coffee shop tables was a reminder of where Britain could improve. But going to a hospital in almost any other part of the world taught me that the National Health Service was probably the single greatest public initiative of all time. The obvious benefit is that it is free, of course, but just as important is that the NHS is a centralised system. Once you're in any hospital, the NHS has a duty of care to take care of you until you recover. Japan is better than many nations, and its public health insurance covers seventy percent of any medical costs. But each hospital is run as a separate business, and none of them are under any obligation take in a new patient. So the kindly old doctor had to call around to various hospitals, virtually begging for them to take me. More alarmingly, my country of origin appeared to be a factor in their decisions. I could only hear one end of the conversation:

'It looks really bad... The testicle has gone deep inside... It might need an operation... He's a foreigner...' There was a long silence, then the doctor's tone became more desperate, almost pleading. 'But he lives in Japan... Yes, he can speak Japanese a little... Britain... Yes, he's from Britain...'

Luckily for me, the UK was apparently on the 'Treatable

Nationalities' list. In a few minutes, the no-nonsense nurse had packed ice around my balls and I was strapped into an ambulance, its sirens blaring as we cut through central Tokyo traffic toward the main university hospital.

It Might Hurt a Bit

'Were you hoping to have children in the future?' the urologist asked. All I could do was grunt through the pain. The doctor continued.

'We're probably going to have to cut it off.'

'I… umm…' It was all too much to take in.

'I will try one more thing. I don't know if it will work, and it might hurt a bit.'

'Let's try,' I begged. I couldn't bear the thought of having my testicle chopped off, and any alternative was worth a shot as far as I was concerned.

Since arriving at the hospital, the doctor had checked me carefully using a sonogram, and expressed his surprise at just how far inside me the testicle had gone. I had received a CAT scan and an MRI and been the subject of numerous X-rays. At each stage, one of the hospital staff would ask me, 'On a scale of one to ten, how strong is the pain?' As this was easily the worst pain of my life, it was natural to give it a ten. But I would soon need to radically rethink that scale.

The doctor felt my stomach area, where the ball had taken up residence. The entire area was a dark purple – the result of internal bleeding. Even the gentlest of touches was enough to make me gasp in agony.

'Ready?' he asked.

I didn't really know what I was supposed to be ready for, but I nodded anyway. He stretched out his arm and laid the palm of his hand on the lump in my abdomen. Then he pushed.

Hard.

Really hard.

I lost control of my senses. I screamed louder than I'd ever screamed before. I used words that I never usually uttered. Tears streamed from my eyes, but I didn't care. The nurse closed the doors, worried about disturbing patients nearby, but I'm not sure it would have helped very much. My screams could probably be heard in the next postal district, let alone the next room.

The doctor paused and I whimpered for him to stop completely. He checked the lump, said something in Japanese, but my ability to decode a foreign language had failed me completely at this point. Then he tried again, this time leaning on my stomach with both palms, placing his entire body weight on my damaged testicle.

'Noooooooooooo!' My voice trailed away, as if my vocal chords had worn themselves out with all the screaming. I gagged on my own saliva and I thought I was going to vomit. My entire body went into uncontrollable spasms and the nurse leaned on me too, trying to keep me still. I became worried that I might hurt her as my limbs jolted wildly in all directions, but there was nothing I could do to prevent it.

It actually took me a few seconds to realise that the doctor had stopped pushing. I had retreated so far inside myself, trying to divorce my mind from my body and all the pain that was shooting

218

through it.

When I regained lucidity, I realised that I was weeping, sobbing helplessly like a young child who had fallen off his bicycle.

'On a scale of one to ten,' the nurse asked, 'how strong is the pain?'

'Ten… thousand,' I blubbered through snot and tears. Then I burst into strange, hysterical laughter.

The nurse attached me to a drip and injected me with pain killers, which seemed a bit late. The doctor explained that he had been partially successful in pushing my ball back into its rightful place.

'Partially?'

'There's too much blood in there now, so I had to stop. Hopefully it will work itself back naturally. If not, we'll have to operate tomorrow.'

They called up to the ward and arranged for a bed to be prepared, then the nurse asked me, 'Is there someone who can bring you some clothes and toiletries? It would help if they speak Japanese too. There are some forms you'll have to fill in. Legal documents.'

I didn't want to leave anything to chance when it came to my testicles. I knew that my mediocre Japanese was not up to the task of reading waivers and consent forms, and in my delirious state I hadn't fully understood what was going on. *Did the doctor say I'd have to stay for a couple of days or a couple of weeks?*

I struggled to think of someone who could help me. My rugby teammates would have been willing to help, I'm sure, but they didn't speak English, so they couldn't assist with the translation. Similarly, my non-Japanese friends were as adept as me at deciphering complicated *kanji*. I considered phoning one of the women I'd been seeing in recent weeks, but I didn't feel comfortable asking for too much from them. Ironically, given the physicality of our relationships, it simply felt too personal to tell them about my injured testicle.

It may have been the drugs that were now coursing through my veins, or the comedown after the adrenalin rush and shock, but I suddenly felt very, very sad. I realised that I was so alone. I had constructed a complex scaffold of friends, lovers and acquaintances. From the outside and in most normal conditions, it gave the illusion of solidity, but there was nothing inside, no central pillar to lean on now that I was being buffeted by a storm. I began feeling sorry for myself, wondering where to turn.

Then the answer hit me and I scrolled through the contact list on my phone. I pressed 'Call'.

'Garett?' the familiar voice asked.

'I've been in an accident.'

She brought me some clothes and picked up toiletries on the way to the hospital. She went through all the admissions forms with me and confirmed the prognosis with the doctor. She even helped me get changed out of my sweaty rugby kit and into pyjamas.

And just like that, Azumi was back in my life.

I lay in bed that night, still attached to a drip and not nearly enough pain killers. Unable to sleep through the deep, throbbing waves of searing agony, I sank into a trough of thoughts and feelings. Would my ball need to be amputated the next day? What affect would that have on me, physically and mentally? Would I be able to have children in the future? What about sex, or even just peeing? The answer to this final question came late in the night, when I finally felt the urge to urinate. Humiliatingly, I had to call the very lovely night nurse to assist me, and she helped adjust my position in bed then gave me a pot with a funnel attached. She watched as I filled it and I felt a slightly misplaced sense of pride when I managed it without any spillage. Embarrassing as it was, I fancied taking this contraption home with me to save me the whole bother of getting up in the night to go to the toilet.

The next morning, the doctor came to see me again, this time with a colleague – plus half a dozen medical students. I was obliged to show my black-and-blue ball sack to all of them, then have the doctor use a biro to lift my penis and allow everyone a better view. The students leaned in, fascinated by my groin, whispering and taking notes diligently. I fought the urge to say 'My face is up here,' and instead asked the doctor if I would need an operation.

After a brief discussion with his colleagues, he finally revealed that his rather primitive attempt to re-position my errant testicle the day before seemed to have worked. I would not need an operation, but I would need to stay in hospital for a week as they monitored my progress and kept an eye on any potential infection. I was so relieved, I could have kissed him, but it was logistically difficult as he was still holding on to my penis.

With that news, my spirits were a lot higher and I began to adjust to life on the ward. My only previous hospital stay had been in Peru when travelling with Azumi a year before. By the shores of Lake Titicaca I fought a battle on two fronts – altitude sickness and salmonella – on a ward that was visibly dirty, forced to use a bed pan that was still spattered with the previous user's excrement. While that experience was a valuable one, learning firsthand the difference between the haves and have-nots in the world, and making friends with locals in ways that I could never have done by staying in hostels, it was also a largely unpleasant memory. Conversely, here in the middle of Tokyo, in one of the best-known hospitals in Japan, the nurses could not do enough for me, checking on my well-being every hour (or more often, at the push of a button), giving me bed baths – which would have been a lot more erotic if my groin wasn't still the shape and colour of an aubergine – and generally making me feel safe and comfortable. When I was well enough to walk, I even received a shampoo and shoulder massage at the salon-style hair washing room. I streamed countless films on the free wi-fi, ploughed through my backlog of podcasts and caught up on all the books I had been meaning to read. I even managed to get some of my Master's thesis written up. Best of all, every evening, Azumi came to see me, bringing snacks and toiletries and double-checking my progress with the nurses or doctor.

But it was the nights that dragged. I struggled to sleep and my mind would begin to wander. Azumi was helping me in my hour of need, but would she stick around afterwards? Was she doing it out of a sense of duty, or because she really cared? Were we back together, or was she simply helping out a friend?

The answer came at the end of my stay. Azumi arrived to help me sign the release forms and pay the hospital fee (despite seventy percent being covered by insurance, it was still about a thousand pounds – a proverbial kick in the balls to go with the literal one). We left together and took the train back to Hirai. We didn't talk about it, and we didn't agonise over the decision; simply, we walked back to her flat – the one that we had shared together. She opened the door, we stepped inside, and I was home.

Enjoy a KFC Christmas

My first Christmas in Japan had been something of a surprise. Surrounded by Buddhist temples and Shinto shrines, I'd expected Christmas to be ignored, but instead I was greeted from October onwards by decorations in every window, seasonal songs in the shops (for some reason, Wham's *Last Christmas* was the favourite), and my conversation school students reminiscing about childhood visits from Santa Claus. Ironically, while many Westerners have become overly cautious about using the word 'Christmas' in official situations, the almost entirely non-Christian Japan holds no such qualms, everyone happily wishing each other a '*Meri Kurisumasu*' despite having no knowledge of what the holiday actually celebrates. This fits in with the broader Japanese pragmatism toward religion. It is considered entirely normal to have a Shinto ceremony for a baby's birth, then a Christian-style white wedding – in which foreign English teachers dress up as ministers on their weekends to perform the 'service' in mock chapels – before using a Buddhist temple for a funeral. As an atheist myself, I quite like this easy-come, easy-go state of affairs. Rather than serving a religion, most Japanese people let religion serve them, and don't get too precious about any of it.

On the other hand, the bastardised version of Christmas can be pretty galling when, despite my atheism, it is one of the most important times of year for me. Rather than being a time for family, the focus in Japan is on young couples going on expensive dates and exchanging gifts on Christmas Eve. It's much nearer to Valentine's Day than Christmas – seen as a romantic, Western thing to do, with restaurants booked up well in advance. So that first Christmas had come as a shock for me, especially when Azumi and I went out for dinner on December twenty-fourth. Seeing this meal as the central point of the holiday, she had been expecting French food, wine and candles; I had given her beer and noodles in a run-down *izakaya*.

My first couple of Christmases in Japan were survivable. My family sent me parcels full of presents, and I held parties with friends, both local and international. But as the time passed, it was one of the few times of year when I felt truly homesick. I wanted to experience a 'real' Christmas again (the term 'real' being subjective, of course, with every nationality believing that their version is the 'real' one). As I had just moved back in with Azumi, we resolved to make this Christmas extra special, so we decided to attempt the impossible: a UK-style Christmas dinner.

Turkey was virtually unheard of in Japan, but chicken was an adequate substitute. Otherwise, we could track down most other items, or get them sent from home. The biggest problem was cooking it all. Japanese kitchens do not come with ovens as standard. The average home will have a tiny fish grill, and a couple of hobs. We also had a toaster oven, about the same size as the fish grill, as well as a very basic microwave. So we blasted the chicken in the microwave first, before cutting it up in order to fit it inside the toaster oven. This gadget came with a confusing safety feature – it shut down whenever it became too hot. So we had to physically turn the dial every fifteen minutes (its maximum cooking time) for the entire afternoon it took to brown the chicken and potatoes, allowing for the occasions that it would be doing precisely nothing as its internal thermometer deemed it too hot to continue cooking. With further vegetables and potatoes 'roasting' in the fish grill, it ended up being one of my proudest achievements when we eventually cobbled together a traditional roast without an oven or a safety net. And it only took five hours.

Still, it felt like we had started a tradition, drinking cider (another rarity in Japan, available in only a few specialist stores) and snacking on cheese and crackers while waiting for everything to – finally – cook.

The odd part of Christmas in Japan revealed itself when we ventured out of the house for a morning walk. While completely natural in a non-Christian country, my brain just could not quite compute the fact that people still went to work, and business went on as normal on December twenty-fifth. Most frustratingly, as Japanese tend to see Christmas Eve as the main event, the carols had ceased and people were taking their decorations down – on Christmas Day! It felt brutal after the long and enthusiastic build-up, as if saying, 'You've had a few hours of fun; don't overdo it.' And the day had only just started. On the plus side, we could go to the supermarket and buy a few extra ingredients for our dinner.

But the weirdest thing of all about Christmas time in Japan is… Kentucky Fried Chicken. While most see the event as primarily romantic, families will also celebrate to some extent. Children generally receive one toy (no more) from 'Santa', and even though it is a regular working day, many have a special meal in the evening. This will invariably include KFC. Like with so many 'traditions' in Japan, it is relatively recent, starting with a marketing push by the American company in 1974. At that time, Christmas was barely celebrated at all in the country, but KFC decided to sell a party bucket of chicken. An advertising campaign convinced the public that it was 'the thing to do' at this time of year, and since then the custom has grown and grown. According to the BBC, over three and a half million Japanese families enjoy a KFC Christmas. The local branch of the restaurant, usually half-full at best, was packed, and a queue of housewives lined around the block for a precious batch of its produce – at increased holiday prices, of course. Many of them would have pre-ordered as far back as October, but the sheer volume of customers ensured a long wait in the cold. For those not lucky enough to get their hands on the real thing, every convenience store in the neighbourhood, as well as the supermarkets, had set up special front-of-shop stalls to sell their own versions of deep fried chicken, along with the other favourite – strawberry shortcake. This particular tradition of light sponge, cream and strawberries pre-dates KFC by a few years, pioneered by the local cake shop chain, Fujiya. It was now ubiquitous to the point that my Japanese friends were unaware that it was not widely eaten in other countries at Christmas. Azumi and I picked up a couple of slices, and it must be said that it made a much lighter alternative to the stodgy fruitcakes and brandy-laced pudding that I had grown up with, and which had always been something of a struggle after a gut-busting roast.

We followed our roast dinner and strawberry cake with gifts, a bottle of wine, and a Terry's Chocolate Orange that my dad had sent over. After a couple of weeks of tentatively being back together, I finally felt that this was permanent. I called the rental company the next day and informed them that I was moving out of my new flat. Azumi then helped me sell my new furniture and appliances online, as well as go through all the city hall bureaucracy once again. The whole process took a month and a half, but it was official: I was back for good.

You're Very Athletic

An unavoidable aspect of December in Japan is the end-of-year party. Called *bounenkai* in Japanese (literally 'forget the year party' – a typically pessimistic term in a country where life is viewed as something to survive rather than enjoy), they are loved and loathed in equal measure. Regarded as sacrosanct in the workplace, all staff must attend, and they are meant to be a time for everyone to celebrate the hard work of the year. This can, of course, be as enjoyable as it sounds; but for many it is yet another drain on their time in an already busy diary. Younger workers, especially, are often expected to subjugate themselves to their elders, pouring drinks, laughing at jokes and generally massaging the egos of middle-aged colleagues – hardly the definition of a fun night out. This tradition of forced jocularity and clearly defined hierarchical roles is deeply ingrained in so much of Japanese life, and only slowly beginning to change.

In fairness, the party at my school was pleasant enough and I guess a lot less boisterous than some events. But it was clear that the younger female teachers felt the need to show willing – refilling older teachers' glasses and putting everyone else's needs ahead of their own. Ms Maki and I almost had a fight over the bottle of beer after I tried to pour for her. She was insistent she fill her own glass, despite already having done it for everyone else. Conversely, I was desperate to be the good guy by allowing her to drink and relax – but in my drunken attempt to show what a gentleman I was, I made her feel a lot more awkward than if I'd just left her to it.

The other memorable moment was when, at the second party, we went to a dark and smoky jazz club (my colleagues loved to go pretty much anywhere expensive). I ended up on a table with three older male teachers, and the question of 'type' came up. It's funny how I never really considered what my ideal type of woman was before coming to Japan. I just saw someone and knew whether I fancied her or not. But for most Japanese people, it's something that has been carefully considered and chosen, like a favourite band or preferred make of breakfast cereal. It's always oddly specific too: *shoulder length hair, with a slight curl at the end, and a small face but big eyes and a softly rounded chin, with a sarcastic sense of humour and an Osaka accent.* It's a wonder that anyone finds a romantic partner, given the miniscule likelihood of actually meeting someone who fits your 'type', and then have that person regard you as *their* type!

During this particular conversation, things took an uncomfortable turn – at least for me – as Mr Nakamura asked us 'Which student is your type?' At first I thought I'd misheard beneath the strains of the saxophone in the background. When he repeated it, I knew that I'd heard correctly. I must have looked like an especially slow goldfish as my mouth gaped open. *Is he really asking me which of our students I fancy?* I looked around, at Mr Kubo and Mr Kaneko, expecting them to be as shocked as I was. Instead, they were both deep in thought.

'I like Akiko chan in the second year,' Mr Kubo piped up after careful analysis. 'She's got a beautiful smile and she's very cheerful, but she's also quite strict on her classmates.'

'She's cute,' said Mr Kaneko, the thickly-bearded Japanese teacher about to reach retirement. 'But she would be too noisy as a girlfriend, always complaining. I like Emika in the third year. She's calm and quiet, but she has beautiful legs.'

Nakamura and Kubo nodded earnestly as if to say 'Good call.' I did what I usually do in these kinds of situations. I excused myself and went to the toilet.

When I came back a few minutes later, they were still in deep and open conversation on the same topic: 'Oh, Mizuho will be a lot prettier in a couple of years.'

'Do you think so? I'd much rather spend time with Izumi chan. She always puts other people's needs first.'

I should say that nobody discussed these girls in blatantly sexual terms, and the three men spoke so openly that I didn't envision them acting on any of these feelings. But I also felt that it was a very dangerous road to travel down – discussing which twelve- to fifteen-year-old girls they found most attractive. It was indicative too of a broader trend in the culture, prominent in TV, films and, especially, manga, where schoolgirls were idealised, objectified and sexualised. Even female friends of mine talked about high school students in very romantic terms, and many longed to go back to those days where they competed to make their skirts as short

231

as possible (by rolling up the waistband) and happily flirted with their teachers.

By normalising all of this behaviour, it was very difficult to judge whether someone was a paedophile, or simply a natural product of a culture that revelled in images of childish cuteness and pubescent sexiness – and often blurred the two. Perhaps more worrying was that young girls, seeing Lolita-style dynamics constantly played out in mainstream media, saw it as normal and even desirable. The J-Pop *idol* scene is based entirely around it, with groups of teenage girls performing what a female Scottish colleague termed a 'rape-me dance' – a blend of gyrating hips and gently chastising finger wagging – for crowds of men in their thirties and forties. I would often see students come to talk with a male teacher in the staffroom, giggling coquettishly and stroking his arm as they tried to ingratiate themselves, perhaps unaware of how this behaviour could be construed.

Far more sinister and explicit manifestations of this seedy undertone occur in fully legal and widely available manga aimed at a young audience that glorify scenes of underage sex and brutal rape, and in photo magazines that show girls as young as seven provocatively posed in bikinis and lingerie (also absolutely fine in the eyes of the law). Again, when talking to Japanese friends – both male and female, and all educated and sensible people – I never heard anyone strongly condemn these publications, as if morally speaking it was merely a bit of a grey area.

Marginally less reprehensible is the tradition of hostess bars. This is a descendent of the geisha culture, and I had experienced it only once before, in my first week in Japan when some co-workers had dragged me to a 'Philippine Pub' in Oyama. I found it a fairly dull couple of hours as I made small talk with a bored-looking woman wearing too much perfume, before discovering that I was paying for her overpriced drinks as well as my own. I spent over half of the cash I'd brought with me to Japan, forcing me to live off cup ramen until my first pay cheque.

I always managed to avoid the places after that, and I remained mystified as to why many male friends seemed so keen on them. Hostesses could in a few cases be bought for more than just chat, but the vast majority of customers were simply paying women to talk to them. I found this impossible to understand – why would I want to spend time with someone who was only there because I was giving her money? It seemed terribly sad to me. Was companionship so difficult to find? Was conversation that much of a rare commodity?

I finally got to experience a hostess bar again, however, at my rugby team's *bounenkai* just after Christmas. Following a three-hour all-you-can-eat-and-drink deal at an *izakaya*, we wandered the streets searching for another bar that could accommodate all twenty of us. Being the festive season, the streets were thronged with drunken groups, stumbling, yelling and vomiting (but without any hint of menace that would probably accompany a similar scene back home), so we were struggling to find a suitable place.

Finally, Kohei took us to a slightly obscure backstreet and his favourite 'snack' – the bizarre euphemism for a hostess bar. I made to go home, but my teammates insisted I join them and I was simply too drunk to protest. We climbed the steps and entered *Café Tropicana Girly Club*.

We sat around the long tables and half a dozen women in their early twenties came to join us. They took orders and mixed drinks for us at a frightening rate – especially as I knew that we would be paying double for everything, and then made cocktails for themselves (on our tab, naturally) while chatting to us enthusiastically. My friends looked delighted, talking at great length about anything and everything. I was particularly surprised to see our coach proudly showing pictures of his university-student daughter while flirting with someone about the same age. In spite of the inherent ickiness, there was kind of a touching purity to the scene. Everybody at the table knew that these girls were just being paid to be nice to us, but they were all willing to go along with the pretence. At last I realised why these pubs were so popular, especially among married middle-aged men. They provided the frisson of excitement and the opportunity to spend time with attractive young women, but the financial nature of the transaction made it safer than if they were chatting to some random person in a bar. On a deeper level, it's a shame that some men feel that they cannot get the same attention at home, but I guess it's better than going to a club to try and pick up a stranger for a one-night stand.

Personally, though, I just could not get excited about this paid friendliness. As much as I wanted to believe that the compliments about my native-speaker-like Japanese ability, obvious sporting prowess and near-perfect film star looks were completely true, it was all too forced. Every few minutes, the hostesses would perform musical chairs and finally I got the chance to talk to the youngest of the group, Anna. I discovered that she had just started working there, and this explained why she came across as much more natural than the others. She didn't emit a hollow laugh at every attempted joke, and she didn't hide the fact that she was tired. She told me that she was trying to save up money for college, and this job paid well, but the late hours were hard and she wasn't sure how long she would stay there. I told her that I didn't have much experience of hostess bars so I was interested to know what they were like. I think she was disarmed by my frankness – I was the only customer who wasn't playing the game – and she appeared to open up to me. She said that most customers were pretty nice but some could 'Touch, touch, touch.' One advantage was that she could sometimes meet people who could give her advice about university and her future career, but her family were worried about her being out all night. I was finally beginning to relax and enjoy the real conversation when one of her fellow hostesses sat nearby and Anna immediately clammed up, as if worried that she would be caught speaking too freely. Her mouth clicked into a false smile, and her voice went up a couple of octaves to the cutesy, nasal pitch that hostesses, shop staff and pop stars seemed to think was attractive. She touched my very average bicep. 'You're very athletic. I bet you're the star player in the team.'

I settled my bill (five times the amount I'd paid in the previous bar) and ran to catch my last train home.

Work-Life Balance

Just like the beginning of every term, the first day back after the winter break was short and mercifully relaxed. There was a morning assembly and the usual barked platitudes from the Principal. Then, after a short homeroom class, the children went home before lunch and the teachers prepared for upcoming classes.

We enjoyed a special lunchbox of *sekihan* – rice boiled with azuki beans to give it a reddish colour, a staple at New Year and other celebrations – as well as some other foodstuffs that I couldn't name.

Then there was a special lecture by a Board of Education representative on the topic of 'Work-life balance'. The Japanese are of course famous for working long hours, and things are no different in a junior high school. A full-time teacher will usually arrive around seven thirty a.m., or earlier if they run a sports club. Lunch is eaten with the students in their classroom so there is no break to speak of throughout the school day, then after classes there are numerous meetings or club activities, as well as lesson planning and marking. Therefore, most teachers do not leave the school until seven or eight in the evening.

The holidays do not give much respite. Most clubs continue to meet every day, and there are also residential training camps and more staff meetings, meaning that even during the six-week summer vacation, most of my colleagues felt lucky to grab a few days' break.

This kind of schedule is nothing out of the ordinary in a country where 'overwork' is deemed a legitimate cause of death by doctors. And that's not including the high number of suicides among employees who simply cannot take the constant strain of long days and few holidays.

While it is absolutely true that Japanese workers tend to spend excessive hours at their offices compared to people in other developed countries, productivity is very low. One of the most common words I heard in Japan was *Ganbatte*. There isn't a satisfactory English translation for this word. Sometimes it means 'good luck', sometimes 'try harder', sometimes 'keep going', but it is used constantly. The sentiment is intended to be positive, to keep fighting even when the chips are down, but I can't help feeling there's an almost cowardly edge to it: there's no need to stop and think, no need to question or reflect or try to do better, no need to find another way; just grit your teeth and carry on – *ganbatte*. So office staff spend hour upon hour at their place of work, the point being not necessarily to achieve anything, but simply to look busy, to show that they are *ganbatte*-ing. In my previous job at a conversation school, the admin staff would usually arrive early and leave late, always looking suitably harried as they buzzed around to complete their tasks. But throughout most of the day, they would work slowly and steadily through their various jobs, happy to stop and chat and occasionally browse the internet. As I got to know the staff better, I learned that they had to phone the head office to inform

238

them whenever they opened and closed the school. Therefore these workers felt pressure to arrive and leave at the most extreme times possible, giving their managers the impression of *ganbatte*. The flipside of this was that they looked genuinely exhausted, spending fourteen-hour days at work with one-hour commutes either side. They were constantly downing little brown bottles of quasi-medicinal energy drinks (rows and rows of different varieties available in any convenience store), sometimes dozing off at their consoles, and not getting much work done until the last-minute rush at the end of the day. Speaking to friends, this was a fairly common situation: giving 'facetime' to their bosses by sitting at their desks as long as possible, but unable to concentrate due to exhaustion, and seeing their families only a few minutes each day.

And even though Japan's labour laws are quite worker-friendly, with clear rules about overtime and holidays (as I had learned when trying to fight the dispatch company's underhand tactics), everybody simply ignores them. In fact, the biggest pressure often comes not from the bosses, but from the employees. A good friend of mine worked for Japan Rail, the major national train company. She said that she was going to lose her holidays because she had carried them over too many years and they would eventually expire. I suggested she use them for a long vacation. She said that she couldn't do that because it would leave her department short staffed.

'But surely it's your manager's job to sort it out and get someone else to cover?' I countered, naively. She just looked confused, unable to comprehend such a thing. As far as she was concerned, she would be letting the side down by taking her rightful days off, so a multi-billion-dollar corporation got weeks of free work out of her, not through explicit coercion but due to peer- and self-induced pressure. Similarly, my rugby teammate's wife took maternity leave, then when she returned to work she was the victim of disparaging comments from colleagues who felt that she had taken too much time off – to have a child!

Progress is occurring at a glacial pace. Japan has more national holidays than most other developed countries, with a fifteenth date added to the calendar recently, compared to eight in England and Wales, and eleven in the US. And more and more workplaces were having talks like the one that we were receiving on work-life balance.

It was of course a sop, a tick-the-box exercise so that the Board could report to the government that they were taking care of their employees. The well-meaning speaker read from a manual then gave us a quiz where we were asked questions like 'Is it important to take regular breaks during a working day?' or 'Is it better to spend weekends doing leisure activities with your family or completing paperwork?' Best of all, she then gave us another sheet of paper (every meeting in Japan comes with at least ten pages of photocopied handouts) listing a schedule for a 'Work-Life Balance Class' – with sessions every Saturday morning! I could imagine the conversations at home: 'Sorry, love, I know we never get to spend time together and the kids barely recognise me, but I really need to attend this seminar at the weekend so I can improve my work-life balance.'

While not necessarily intentional, I couldn't help thinking that by providing these classes, the employer was subtly placing more pressure on the employees' shoulders. Never mind giving people the holidays that they were entitled to by law, never mind banning unpaid overtime, never mind cutting some of the admin tasks that teachers had to do (which in other countries would usually have been covered by secretarial staff); instead it suggested that work-life balance was the responsibility of the workers, and if they couldn't sort it out, well, they only had themselves to blame.

After the lecture, I asked Ms Ikuta if she would be going to the Saturday classes. She sighed, dispirited. 'I suppose I ought to.'

Yamada Kun

By now, I was long accustomed to the morning routine. The crush of commuters on the Sobu line, then the brief, refreshing walk near the sumo stadium at Ryogoku, and the hot tang of vending machine coffee before I entered the underground train station. Even in the hubbub of central Tokyo, I got to recognise many of the faces I saw each day, able to judge if I was ahead of schedule or behind, based on when I passed particular people on the street.

This Thursday morning, I was running late so after alighting from the train I broke into a jog over the bridge leading to my school. I arrived just in time, slipped on my indoor shoes and said good morning to Ms Furukawa, one of the admin staff who was usually so chatty but now hesitated before a muttered greeting. Irritated by her lack of friendliness, I bounded upstairs and ran into Ms Maki just outside the staffroom. 'Garett!' she exclaimed, then looked lost for words. I worried that I was in trouble.

'We've had some bad news,' she said, and a tear ran down her cheek.

Yamada Daiki was a fairly typical example of a third year student in the school. He showed up on time, went through all the motions, but rarely gave any more effort than was absolutely necessary. In the case of lessons with Ms Hasebe, that was zero. My relationship with Yamada kun consisted of me nagging him to at least finish the first section of the worksheet I'd just given him. When he'd finally deigned to do that, I would push him to complete the next section. For this reason I doubt that he liked me, though his demeanour suggested that he didn't like anyone all that much, rarely smiling and often sighing. However, he had a decent bunch of friends and no apparent enemies. He resembled most of his classmates in his love of reading comics and drawing pictures (usually in class!) and did his best not to stand out in any way. In short, he was a teenager.

He came from an affluent family living in one of the luxury skyscrapers that towered over the school grounds and always scared me whenever an earthquake hit. His mother was on the Parents and Teachers Association and a very kind woman who would bring sweets for the staff and always had time for a chat.

The previous day Yamada kun had come to school as normal, then dozed and doodled his way through classes. In the afternoon he made the short journey home, accompanied by his friends, as was their routine. None of them saw any hint of what was to come as he said goodbye and rode the lift to his family's apartment on the forty-second floor.

Later that evening he had an argument with his older sister, apparently over an iPad. It was a heated quarrel but not bad enough to cause any great concern, just the kind of squabble so common among siblings. Angry, Yamada kun went to his bedroom then stepped out onto the balcony. Nobody knows how long he stood there; whether he noticed the icy breeze on one of the coldest nights of winter; whether he gave a moment's thought to the panorama of Tokyo lights. All we know is that he climbed up onto the railing and somehow found inside him the despair, bitterness and courage to let go, falling ninety metres to the pavement below.

A woman walking her dog found the body, she called the police and they informed the family and school. Yamada Daiki was declared dead at the hospital.

I first thought Ms Maki must have been mistaken. 'Yamada kun killed himself.' It was just too outrageous. I groped around for another interpretation besides the most obvious and most awful. Was it a joke? An error in her English? An exaggeration, like when we say 'I killed myself to finish that report'?

I went to the sports hall where the students and teachers were already assembled. The Principal was explaining what had happened. It was real. A few students were sobbing but most stood as I did, in complete shock. The Principal told them that we must be strong as a school and as a community, then broke down in tears. The man who had seemed such a tyrant back on my first day was now weeping in front of hundreds of people. A moment's silence was called and it was the first chance I had to try and take it all in. Yamada had jumped. Yamada was dead. I don't know why but I took a deep breath, not wanting to cry. Mr Arakawa, the Vice-Principal, announced that lessons would go on as normal.

'Ganbatte,' he said. 'Ganbatte.'

Keep going.

At that moment, I didn't really feel like doing that, and I

doubt if Yamada kun's friends and classmates were any different. But five minutes later, I found myself in the bizarre situation of putting on a fake smile and practising 'I like spaghetti' with a first year class, in the shadow of Yamada kun's building.

It was like a surreal dream, teaching classes as well as we could then returning to the staffroom for more updates. We didn't know the full reasons yet so, as well as the genuine shock and grief, a lot of teachers must have been worrying about their own futures. A year earlier in another part of Tokyo there had been a teenage suicide caused by school bullying. The Principal in that particular case was fired, but not before having to make a very contrite and humiliating apology in front of the nation's TV cameras. Yamada kun's death had been reported on the morning news and the media was bombarding the school with phone calls and visits, a teenage suicide whetting their appetites for a juicy scandal behind it. It was his mother who made a statement to the police and journalists, stressing that the cause was absolutely *not* bullying. This was an incredibly selfless act on what must have been the worst day of her life. As an active member of the PTA she would have known all the implications involved but, within twenty-four hours of losing her son, she took the time to make clear the reasons for the tragedy and save a lot of careers. A family argument not likely to sell as many newspapers as bullying, the media stopped calling. Luckily for them, on the same day an eighteen-year-old judo wrestler was beaten to death by his coach and fellow *dojo* members in an overzealous initiation rite, so they could leap onto that story instead.

I couldn't face rugby practice that evening and Azumi was working late so I just sat in silence in my flat, trying to make sense of it all. Did he really mean to jump? Had he thought about it before? Was it merely an 'I'll show you' moment from a headstrong adolescent? Was there something else troubling him? Was it truly all about a stupid iPad? Or was it a cumulation of things?

I found it odd that no-one had mentioned the pertinent detail that he had received some exam results the day of his death. While he was never a student who seemed unduly concerned about his education, much preferring to sleep or chat, the pressure must have been immense for all of the third years at that time. By the end of the term they needed to select their prospective senior high schools, effectively shaping the rest of their lives in a society where the names of people's high schools and universities are relevant throughout their careers. Of course, test results played the major part in deciding students' fates and – after so long being pampered and essentially given free rein over whether to study or not, even whether to come to school or not – there must have come a moment of awful realisation for every student when they saw their grades slip further and further (as many had) and their opportunities became slimmer and slimmer. While we don't know for sure Yamada's state of mind, there was an air of palpable relief in the staffroom at the news that the suicide had nothing to do with the school, and the chance for some much-needed soul-searching was swept quietly under the carpet.

The knowledge that there would never be any definite

answers, and that perhaps it was an entirely senseless deed, did not stop me from pondering every possibility, but most of all I thought about his family, and especially his poor older sister who had apparently caused him to jump.

The next day was the same, an atmosphere thick with gloom, but everyone pretending that things were normal. The only clue to a tragedy was the presence of counsellors, quietly ensconced in the meeting room. It was quite frightening how quickly most of the students seemed to adjust. I suppose the first and second years didn't know Yamada very well, but the third years, even his classmates, continued in their self-centred way, laughing, chatting and sleeping like it was any other day. I'm sure for some it was just bravado, others shock, but a disturbingly large number really didn't show any emotion at all, and I seriously questioned their capacity to care for other human beings at all. It's difficult to know if they just happened to be bad kids, or if the way they'd been treated for nearly three years at the school (and possibly many years previously) had shaped their attitudes. By always being allowed to do whatever they wanted – be it napping through lessons, ignoring teachers' requests or disrupting other people's attempts to learn – and never being taught that sometimes we have to consider other people's feelings, they can't really be blamed for developing a view of the world as a system designed solely for their own immediate wants.

Understandably, Yamada's class teacher, Ms Kitahara, was in a terrible state. She had to clear out his desk, console his close friends and visit the family, and all while continuing to teach her regular classes. Her skin was pale, her eyes were red and she visibly aged within forty-eight hours, but that didn't stop students pestering her about the brass band club she supervised. It was a miracle she didn't just give up and leave.

As for me, I cruised through lessons, still shaking with disbelief but just about managing to teach. In an afternoon elective class none of the students were in the mood for serious study, and, as I wasn't either, I said we would just play a word game. It was only after I had chalked the dashes on the blackboard then begun drawing the gallows that I realised a game of Hangman wasn't the most appropriate in the circumstances. I somehow managed to morph the picture into Darth Vader's face before the bell rang and we could finally go home.

I took the Metro train to Ryogoku and decided to take a break at Starbucks (the only guaranteed non-smoking coffee shops in Tokyo). It felt good to sit somewhere bright, warm and full of energy, even if I was just a spectator on the fringes. Through the window I watched schoolchildren and office workers walk in and out of the station. It was Friday evening so there was a thrill of freedom in the air. Some commuters were on their way home for a weekend of TV, golf or sleep (something that for rest-deprived Japanese workers is considered a *bona fide* hobby); others were in excited groups, Happy Hour just beginning at the local bars. Another week, that could have been me, but instead I just nursed my mocha, not caring that the cream was curdling on top. The vastness of what Yamada had done was almost incomprehensible and I kept replaying my imagined view from his balcony, across the Tokyo skyline then down to the pavement. But despite all that, these people outside could still laugh, could still adjust their hair before a date, could still rush to get the train as if it were the only thing that mattered. A young life was finished, a family was destroyed, and hundreds of others affected, but the world didn't stop. I was comforted by this thought, but also appalled that an entire lifetime of possibilities was denied and all for nothing.

I finished the cold, syrupy dregs of coffee and made the final leg of my journey home on the hectic Sobu line. From Hirai station I weaved through the crowds to my small block of flats. On auto-pilot, I typed in the code on the new keypad lock, the only modern convenience in an otherwise aging building. I walked up the winding stairs to the fourth floor. I fumbled past the phone, USB stick and box of mints in my trouser pocket, eventually finding my keys. I opened the door, entered and kicked off my shoes. The door eased shut behind me and I breathed in the silence.

Then, like a tidal wave, it happened in an instant: a wail of grief emanating from the depths of my lungs. It was unstoppable, absolutely primal and followed by more. I fell against the wall as my legs gave way and I let out more cries. The poor neighbours must have been horrified but at that moment they didn't exist to me. All I could think of was Yamada, his family and, most of all, the complete *waste*. Two days of holding everything together, of *ganbatte*-ing, had finally ended and I screamed out the pain and confusion for half an hour. When my mouth was dry and my voice couldn't function anymore, I slid to the wooden floor. I'm not sure how long it was before I finally found enough power to stumble to the sofa, sit down and breathe again, but it was pitch black.

Salt-Flavoured Suit

On Saturday there was the pre-funeral ceremony when people could offer their condolences to the family and pray for the deceased. This was my first experience of a Japanese funeral but I was aware that I would have to wear a black suit, black tie and white shirt. I had bought a new suit for Allan and Ryoko's wedding just a few months earlier and, with rare foresight, had got it in black, just in case. What I hadn't considered was that while a slim-fitting style might have been rather dashing at a wedding, it wasn't as easy to carry off at a funeral, and I had to suck everything in just to fasten the jacket buttons. I felt faintly foolish as my shirt appeared to be fighting its way out of the suit, but it was too late to change so I made my way to school. Ms Hasebe had told me that the teachers would be leaving for the ceremony at half past five so I planned to arrive in plenty of time to grab the packet of tissues from my desk, put on my black tie and simply gather my thoughts before the ordeal ahead. So it came as a surprise to see all of the staff waiting at the front gate of the school when I got there thirty minutes early, Mr Kubo barking at me to hurry up. Hasebe had misinformed me again. As if on cue the rain began to fall while we walked to a local park – the meeting point for the students – and I struggled to knot my tie without the aid of a mirror. Ms Maki lent me her umbrella (something else I hadn't had time to pick up from the staffroom) but otherwise nobody spoke to me during the walk. Many teachers seemed bewildered that I came, a mix of gratitude and suspicion in their loud whispers on my arrival. Even though I spent more one-to-one time with students than any other teacher, some staff were amazed that I would even know their names. It was a ridiculous notion but one that tallied with the view that I wasn't a real teacher and not a full member of the team, therefore I couldn't possibly know what was going on. My mood became even darker.

The procession of children and teachers arrived at the funeral home. I'm convinced that the Japanese economy is kept alive by obligatory gift-giving, and each of us presented an envelope of cash as we entered. As with weddings, funerals are hugely expensive so these cash donations are vital to finance them; the only winners are the undertakers. Like weddings, the money must be wrapped in a traditional envelope with complex folding instructions; unlike weddings, the notes must not be new, causing me to scrunch up my annoyingly crisp five thousand yen bill. As we reached the front of the queue where funeral workers were waiting, Ms Maki explained some of the protocol – what to say and what to write in the guest book. I handed over the envelope in both hands, bowing deeply. Ms Maki yelped and rushed to snatch it out of my hands.

'It's the wrong way up!' She corrected it, and gave it back to me to pass to the receptionist. I shouldn't be too harsh on Ms Maki – she was the only colleague all day to show me any respect – but the friendly receptionist, who dealt with this situation on a daily basis, probably didn't care too much how I passed it, her understanding smile showing that she knew I wasn't a veteran of these events. By grabbing it from me and explaining breathlessly, it just made me self-conscious and ashamed, about the only two negative emotions I wasn't already feeling. It also made me very nervous as we waited to enter the main hall and pay our respects to the family and Yamada kun's coffin.

When some teachers had visited the day before, the casket had been opened. This has always struck me as macabre, even after the most peaceful of deaths, let alone after a forty-two-floor jump, and I was worried about how poor Yamada kun would look. Thankfully, the coffin was now closed and shrouded in flowers. A photo portrait tied in a traditional black ribbon rested on top.

I tried to watch the order of rituals through the crowd as we moved further up the line: bow to the family, bow to the coffin; take powdered incense from one pot, touch it to the forehead then add it to another pot, and repeat twice more; bow to the family again. I hoped I'd done it correctly but had half an eye on Ms Maki in case she'd run across and grab me if I picked up too much incense. I think I got it right.

The sight of the family broke my heart. The mother was sobbing gently, the father and sisters nodding courteously to every one of the hundreds of mourners. Lives changed forever.

In the lobby outside there was a small presentation on a table. Alongside more pictures of Yamada kun (none of him smiling; he was always a glum boy) there were drawings he had made, quite possibly in English class. Most affecting, there were packets of his favourite snacks, including Black Thunder chocolate biscuits, the same cheap but tasty variety that I often bought. Their ordinariness was a sad reminder of the fragility of life. Three days earlier he could have been eating those. Now he was gone.

One of the PTA members was stood next to me and she asked me upstairs to a small wake they had arranged. I went up and nibbled on a sushi roll and pretended to drink the beer she gave me. I appreciated her taking care of me and stayed long enough to be polite, but I longed to get some fresh air.

Back on the ground floor I was asked for the numbered ticket I had received when giving money. In exchange for this I received a bag of presents, a traditional thank you.

The teachers were grouped around the front door and Ms Hasebe asked where I had been.

'I went to the wake,' I explained. Hasebe sniffed her disapproval.

'That's only for very close family, not you.'

'Well, the organisers invited me and I felt it would be rude to refuse.'

'No, no. It's just for relatives.'

'There were lots of people there. The Vice-Principal was there, plus Ms Fukuda. And the PTA invited me. It would have been very impolite to say no.'

As usual, facts were no argument against Hasebe. I was the stupid foreigner sure to make a *faux pas* if she weren't there to look out for me, therefore I must have made a mistake. This was the story she then took to any teacher who would listen. I don't think I've ever felt so alone.

On the train ride home I looked inside the gift bag. Expectedly, everything was beautifully wrapped and it took some time to peel off the thick paper. Inside I found some strips of dried seaweed and a pot of green tea powder, standard fare on these occasions. Mysteriously, there was also a small sachet of salt. I had time to ponder as the underground train inexplicably stopped between stations, an extremely rare occurrence on the clinically efficient transport system (the very next day after the Atomic Bomb hit Hiroshima, the trams were running again). Was the salt to accompany the seaweed? An addition to the tea? Neither use appealed to me. More importantly, I thought about the funeral itself, to be held the following day. When the teachers were discussing arrangements, they hadn't involved me. Ms Hasebe, usually so keen to laden me with every detail – however skewed – of schedules, had just said, 'See you on Monday.' I knew that if I decided to show up, I would have to face more dubious looks and be reminded yet again that I wasn't part of the community, no matter that I worked with everyone full-time, and no matter that I knew Yamada kun more closely than most of the staff. I knew, too, that I would cause a nuisance for those kinder souls who felt the need to take care of me, cover my every move, just in case I did something outrageously foreign and stupid. Azumi had told me that – duty-wise – I needn't go to both ceremonies but, honestly, I wanted to. However, my being there would cause more distraction for others and more upset for me in being so clearly excluded. As the train chugged back to life, I decided not to attend.

Belatedly, I arrived home and the wave hit me again. This time I knew it was coming and didn't feel so shocked by the moans bursting from deep inside; I just let them out and fell into Azumi's arms.

I then discovered what the salt was for. Azumi insisted on scattering it over my shoulders and shoes as a cleansing act before I stepped over the threshold, salt believed to ward away the bad spirits that would surely be lingering at a funeral home. Now I was spooked up as well as depressed.

I got changed out of my tight, salt-flavoured suit and forced down some dinner. I turned on the television and watched my favourite football team lose a vital game in the very last minute. I didn't care.

A Scene from Blade Runner

The next few weeks were strange. The teachers and students went through the motions in a kind of collective shock. Occasionally, Ms Kinukawa would break down in tears for a few seconds, then apologise and get back to work.

Slowly, coldly, brutally, life went back to normal. For all the grief, things couldn't stop. There were still lessons to teach, tests to take, lives to live.

Azumi and I resolved to make the most of every weekend. We took trips to Niigata, just ninety minutes from Tokyo, where I learned to ski in a class of eight-year-olds. We went to the Izu peninsula to experience the stark beauty and colourful seafood of a fishing village in winter. And we hosted my old college friend Paul and his wife Maddy as they stopped over for a couple of days on the way to visiting her cousins in Australia.

With Paul and Maddy, we ticked off all the the usual spots that visitors enjoy: Kamakura and its massive bronze statue of Buddha, Asakusa's bright red shrines, and the modern hedonism of Shibuya. Their favourite place, though, was Yurakucho, the less salubrious area that flanks the high-class Ginza shopping district.

Spring had come early and it was pleasantly warm, even as the sun dipped behind the bullet trains whizzing over our heads. The railway arches shuddered with every passing locomotive, but no-one seemed to notice in the dozens of little restaurants that belched out smoked and steam, stinging our eyes but tantalising our taste buds. We could take our pick of cuisine: Chinese dumplings, Korean barbecue, German sausage. But the area's most famous dish was *yakitori* – chicken skewers.

We found a free 'table' just in front of a whitewashed and functional bar. I use quotation marks as it wasn't a table *per se*, but a couple of plastic yellow beer crates with a wooden board placed on top. Similarly, our 'chairs' were beer crates too. An interesting aspect of aesthetics in Japan is the frequent juxtaposition of ultra-modern chic and primitive improvisation. It's messy, confusing, and fascinating. In any part of Tokyo, you can never be sure what you might find around the next corner.

This street was gritty and greasy, cheap beer sloshing in chunky tankards, conversation louder than usual, and the skewers – of vegetables and pork and potatoes, as well as chicken – kept on coming from the elderly owner of the bar. He clapped his hands and yelled loudly as he tried to drum up more trade, although the place was already packed to bursting. It was raucous and dirty, yet the clientele was decidedly upmarket, businesspeople unwinding after work, and well-dressed shoppers relaxing after a day at Louis Vuitton and Tiffany's.

Day turned to the magic hour of dusk, then a blue-lit neon night. We watched the passers-by, like a fashion show of high-end brands, and Paul and Maddy were happy to see a few women in kimono too, clip-clopping past on dainty sandals. Reflected in the windows of the shop opposite was the *Shinkansen* bullet train, hurtling above us on its way to Kyoto and drowning out conversation for a few seconds at a time. With swirls of smoke pumping from extractor fans and cigarettes, Paul was more correct than he realised when he remarked, 'It's like a scene from *Blade Runner.*' In fact, director Ridley Scott had used this area as one of his inspirations for the sci-fi classic.

Just as we were about to leave – full on beer and chicken – a couple of men carrying some kind of large recording device approached our table. They asked if we could answer a few questions for a live radio show and they handed me a mobile phone attached to the contraption. I was put through to one of the most famous pop stars in the country, which thrilled Azumi. He cleared his throat and used his best English: 'Can I ask you a question?'

'Go ahead,' I said, expecting the usual bland interrogation about my favourite Japanese food or how long I had been in the country.

'Have you ever tried Polynesian sex?'

'S-Sorry?'

'Polynesian sex. Have you done it?'

This was followed by further enquiries about tantric sex, cyber sex, and… well, you get the idea. It turns out that, despite a squeaky clean image in his music and TV work, his late-night radio show was well known for its risqué themes. Once the surprise had worn off, I remembered that he was romantically involved with one of my favourite actresses. When I mentioned her name, the conversation stopped abruptly, the production assistant yanked the phone out of my hands and they moved away fast. Apparently intimate questions about my sex life were completely fine, but any mention of his girlfriend was strictly off limits.

I've dined out on the story ever since, although I always need to edit the contents a little when telling my students about it.

The following day, I accompanied Paul and Maddy out to Narita Airport and we hugged our goodbyes as I had done with so many friends and family. No matter how often I did this, I never grew used to it, and the journey back felt especially bleak, the inevitable melancholy after the brief, intense high of their visit.

I'm not sure why, but I got off the train a couple of stops early and took a walk along the Edo River. The morning had been warm and bright, but it was gloomy now, the faint rumble of distant thunder in the air. This was an iconic waterway, the old economic centre of the capital, but like so many historical spots of Japan, its development since then had been purely pragmatic. Its banks were now covered in concrete, and a major highway snaked above the riverside on an overpass. This was probably why it was so underused by Sunday afternoon strollers, in spite of the specially built pedestrian walkway.

I ambled along, lost in thoughts of home and Japan. The cars roared overhead, and the threat of an impending storm rustled through the strands of long grass that poked out bravely between tarmac and breeze blocks. These ominous sounds morphed into a kind of white noise that shut out the real world. The only people I saw were homeless men. Far rarer than most other countries, homelessness still exists in many Japanese cities. This pathway, sheltered by the raised highway, proliferated with little improvised huts made from balsa wood, cardboard and blue canvas. I found the sight quite profound. Each hut had a cardboard front doormat, where a pair of sandals waited. Even here, indoor shoes were required. Similarly, most of the shacks were fringed with little pot plants, as if the owners had a pride in their appearance, high standards even in the lowest of circumstances.

I had bought my ticket for a trip to the UK in the spring holiday, just a couple of weeks away. I was excited, of course. I could see my family again, and I would be able to understand everything around me (something akin to developing a superpower after living in a place where my grasp of conversations, signs and menus was, at best, one step behind everybody else's). I planned to eat all the roast lamb that my stomach would allow and watch as much non-Japanese TV as I could squeeze in. It would be thrilling and different.

Then it hit me.

Different.

It would be *different.*

After half a decade in Japan, and especially the past year, taking the first tentative steps into a truly local community, my perspective had changed. I was from Britain, and my roots and family would always be there.

But whether I liked it or not, Japan had become… home.

Is This My Salary?

The premature arrival of spring brought the cherry blossoms earlier than usual. I often got frustrated at the way that Japanese people thought their country was alone in having not one, not two, not even three, but... *four* seasons. If locals were discussing the differences between Japan and other nations (something that was surprisingly common, with the national psyche teetering somewhere between crippling insecurity and arrogant exceptionalism), one of the most common examples of their country's uniqueness was just that: 'Japan has four seasons.' When I revealed that Britain had four seasons too, as did hundreds of countries around the world, many acquaintances would look at me suspiciously, convinced that I must be lying. What Japan *does* have, however, is a deep appreciation for each season and a strong urge to mark them through festivals, food and clothing. This can occasionally be amusing, like when every September Azumi decks herself out in the latest autumn fashions – thick sweaters and knit hats – even though it's nearly thirty degrees celsius. She then needs to repeatedly mop the streams of sweat from her face, while asking me, 'Aren't you cold in that T-shirt? It's autumn!' But this regard for changing seasons manifests itself most impressively in springtime, when the pink blossoms bloom on the cherry trees that seem to line every street in every town. It really is a spectacular sight, and with it comes the *hanami* – flower viewing –

263

party. Every park and riverside becomes swathed in tarpaulin leisure sheets and wool blankets, and friends and colleagues gather to eat picnics and drink copious amounts of beer and *sake*. Such is the association between alcohol and *hanami,* most beer companies change their packaging around March and April, pink blossoms adorning every can of Kirin or Asahi.

My first experiences of the cherry blossom season in Japan were slightly disappointing. I had previously envisaged balmy evenings under the tree branches, everyone in shirt sleeves as they toasted the season. But that first spring had been cold – at least after sundown – and my friends and I shivered in coats and scarves as we clung to our ice cold beers and tried not to be the first person to say, 'Bugger this, let's find a nice warm bar.'

But this particular year was a rarity with unbroken sunny days and mild evenings, and it was very pleasurable to sit in the park near the school, sharing sashimi, sandwiches and *edamame* with my colleagues as we looked forward to the upcoming holiday – and the completion of the school year.

For once, we were able to wrap up the after-school meetings and test marking much earlier than usual, and I joined a group of teachers who went ahead to stake a spot in the park. Thankfully, in this residential area, it was not such a tough task, but in the busier parts of Tokyo, office juniors are often sent out early in the morning in order to claim a drinking space for their company's evening party.

We stretched out on the floor, chatting to each other and the passing students, who seemed completely unperturbed to see their teachers swigging cans of beer and *shochu* in the park. I was impressed with how comfortable they were to come and talk to us, which was strangely at odds with their usual reticence to speak. It was as if once the shackles of the school environment were lifted, then they were free to relax and be themselves.

Parents, too, came over to say hello, with one mother donating a free supply of dumplings from her nearby shop. One of my favourite third years, Mami chan, approached with her mum, and I felt the need to look at anywhere but her chest – this was the girl whose breasts I had complimented so enthusiastically at the post-Culture Festival party. Her mother showed no signs of holding a grudge, thank goodness, and made a beeline for me, looking on proudly as Mami chatted to me in English about being accepted into one of the top high schools in the city.

Slowly, our numbers increased as other teachers finished up their day's work, and I began to feel quite sentimental. The dispatch company who employed me had not offered me a new contract for the next school year, and following my arguments with them I did not feel confident about staying with them, or continuing at the same school even if I was still employed. The thought made me sad. Things had not been perfect, by any means, and I still felt like an associate member of the team; however, this was the first time that I had worked in a completely Japanese environment, after my years of conversation school jobs alongside other foreign teachers, and I hated the thought of having to start again elsewhere. And sitting in that warm twilight glow, pink blossom drifting onto my shoulders and conversation flowing as fast as the beer… Well, I longed for the opportunity to continue, to try and build on this next year, to truly become a part of the community.

As if on cue, Mr Arakawa, the Deputy Head, arrived at the party. He looked serious, still in work mode while everybody else was loosening their neckties. I guessed that some issue had cropped up with a student or parent. Then I realised he was heading towards me.

'Garett, Garett,' he blurted, short of breath. 'Can you come back to the school? The Board of Education wants to talk to you.'

My co-workers looked concerned, but not nearly as concerned as I was. What had happened? Had there been some complaint about me? Had I done something terribly wrong?

Mr Arakawa and I rushed back to the school, which was empty now. 'It's OK,' he kept repeating, in a flustered way that made it seem anything but OK.

We changed into our indoor shoes, an annoying hindrance when I wanted to find out what was going on as soon as possible. We ran up the stairs and Mr Arakawa unlocked the door to the staffroom. My head was spinning now, the stress and physical exertion following so quickly after four cans of strong lager.

He ushered me to sit down next to his desk at the head of the room, then dialled a number on his phone.

After what seemed like an age, he was put through to someone – I still didn't know who – and the small talk seemed interminable. There was then a hurried conversation, too fast for me to follow, in which my name came up repeatedly. Finally, the Vice-Principal passed me the phone.

'*Moshi moshi*,' I said; the requisite phone greeting that always sounded delightfully childlike to my ears.

'Hello?' came a reply, in English. 'Is that Garett Wilson?'

It was the man in charge of scheduling at the Board of Education. I never did learn his name. 'Your company says that you may not be working with us next year.'

'Umm, no. I mean, I don't know. I haven't heard anything.'

'So you want to continue?'

'Well, yes.'

'Oh, that's good. I understand that there were some problems with your contract.'

'Umm, yeah...'

'There will be a different contract next year. It has been agreed with the dispatch company. I faxed a copy to Mr Arakawa.'

My heart sank. If the dispatch company had signed off on it, then the chances were that it worked in their favour – and against mine.

'Right. Well, thank you,' I murmured, and we said our goodbyes.

Mr Arakawa had the fax in his hand and passed it to me. I skimmed through the contract – in Japanese – trying to find something I understood among the hundreds of *kanji* characters. I saw what looked like working hours, and Mr Arakawa confirmed that they were my new daily start and end times as agreed with the agency: *eight to five thirty.* I sighed. Longer hours than now, and exactly what I'd tried to fight against when I had gone up against the company.

Then my eyes were drawn to another figure.

'Is this my salary?' I asked.

The Vice-Principal nodded.

It was a twenty percent raise.

'And here,' he added, using English. 'Health insurance.' The very thing that I had insisted we get in accordance with our hours and Japanese law.

'Is this for all teachers in the district?'

'Yes.'

I must admit that a selfish part of me was irritated. My peers – Graeme, Rob, Jim, as well as all of the Assistant Language Teachers in primary schools and senior high schools – were going to get the benefits that only I had risked everything for. Then I realised that I was being churlish. After years of being taken advantage of, from now on all of the ALTs in the area would get fair treatment. It was the first Board of Education in Tokyo to offer this to its foreign teachers. I smiled. Mr Arakawa smiled too. There was a small refrigerator in the corner of the staffroom. He opened it and pulled out a six-pack of beer.

'Let's go back to the party, Garett.'

Stand Up, Bow and Sit Down

Just as my first year at the school had begun with well-dressed parents coming for the start-of-term ceremony, so it ended in similar fashion with Graduation.

Beforehand, there were two weeks of rehearsals in which the students had to learn exactly when they should stand up, bow and sit down. Even the act of receiving the graduation certificate was carefully choreographed and practised – each student had to stand straight, then march towards the stage military-style, give a bow to the VIPs from the local government, a bow to the teachers, a bow to the Principal who was handing out the certificate, then reach out with the right hand, then the left, take the certificate with straight arms, take one step back, bow again to the Principal, turn to the audience of peers and parents and bow once more, tuck the certificate neatly under the left arm, before finally returning to their seat. The simple act of accepting a piece of paper was so wrapped in ritual that I felt for the many students who made mistakes then got shouted at by Mr Kubo in front of the entire school.

The teachers all had to pitch in to decorate the sports hall in massive red-and-white striped banners that covered the four walls from top to bottom. Every available chair was commandeered to seat the hundreds of guests and students, and Ms Ikuta was assigned the task of checking that every row was impeccably straight, even using a tape measure to check that each chair was equidistant. The obsession with getting every tiny detail unimpeachably perfect somehow took all genuine meaning out of the occasion. I felt it was really difficult to be moved by this rite of passage and the fact that the graduating students were about to be scattered to schools all over Tokyo; instead, everyone was too terrified of mistiming a bow.

Unlike the start-of-year ceremony, I was now well accustomed to these kinds of occasions, so I felt much more relaxed in the event itself. After a year of assemblies and various ceremonies, I was adept at following the actions of people around me, so I could remain on a kind of auto-pilot as I stood and bowed and clapped in perfect unison with my colleagues.

In all honesty, now that I knew I'd be teaching here again for another year, I thought I'd be glad to see the back of these third years, by far the least likable group in the school. But strangely, as they lined up onstage to sing a syrupy farewell song about their hometown, it occurred to me how many I would really miss. There were certainly a higher proportion of disruptive kids in the year, but in truth it was only four or five in each class. There were also a lot of really lovely students, and as the mums and dads collapsed into sobs, I felt a twinge of sadness too.

When a special certificate was presented to the mother of Yamada kun, only a couple of months after his death, then I was glad that I had packed a handkerchief in my suit pocket. The gruff old Principal wept openly once again as Mrs Yamada, resplendent in a blue kimono, accepted the award with typical grace.

The third years filed out of the hall wailing hysterically, with many of the teachers equally teary. Then the staff and younger kids formed a guard of honour in the playground through which the graduating students cried some more, exchanging hugs with their junior clubmates. Some of the boys ripped the buttons off their uniform jackets and gave them to admiring girls – a tradition at Graduations – and there was a real poignancy to the scene. Most of these children had grown up together, at the same pre-schools and primary schools too, so this was the first time that they would be separated. The cherry blossoms fell to the ground around the school gate, a melancholic pink carpet for the students to walk over as they left everything they knew and ended this chapter in their lives.

As I exited the same gate a few hours later, it was strange to think that I would be back very soon, the new school year beginning just two weeks later. These three terms had been so eventful, challenging me, educating me, and changing my perception of Japan entirely, and I felt like I needed a long holiday to recuperate before starting the whole cycle once again. As it was, I was due to leave Japan the next morning for a two-week trip home, a chance to catch up with family and friends, some of whom I hadn't seen for a year or more.

Before that, though, I had one more thing to do in Tokyo.

The distance between the school and the Metro station was a lot shorter than it had seemed that rainy morning nearly a year ago. It was a still, mild evening, and I was happy to take my time crossing the bridge, watching a lone fishing boat chug upriver. By train it only took fifteen minutes to reach central Tokyo and the Marunouchi business district. For once I fitted in with the office workers milling around me, still dressed in my best suit after the Graduation. As this would be our last meal together for two weeks, I wanted to find somewhere special to take Azumi, and I was spoilt for choice in the ultra-modern chrome-and-glass neighbourhood. I decided on a classy-looking Spanish place and booked a table for two, then I waited at a coffee shop for Azumi to meet me after work.

When she arrived, twenty minutes late, she was clearly stressed, breathing hard and complaining about her overzealous boss.

'Well, forget all that for tonight,' I said. 'Let's go to a nice restaurant. My treat.'

'To be honest, I just fancy having something at home.'

'Oh.'

'Shall we call and get a Pizza Hut?'

This wasn't going quite as I'd planned. 'Go on,' I urged. 'It's our last evening together for a while. I wanted to do something special.'

'Well, alright then. But I really feel like pizza. Shall we try Mario's round the corner?'

Mario's was a perfectly acceptable chain restaurant but, again, not really what I had in mind for a romantic last meal before I left the country.

'Actually, I booked a table at the Spanish place across the road.'

'Booked? Why did you do that?'

272

'Well, I wanted to… Umm… Dunno, really.' I was sure that most men didn't have this much difficulty when trying to take their partner for a posh dinner. 'Let's give it a try anyway.'

In the end, the meal was adequate at best, but the ambience was calm and cosy, all oak panelling with legs of Iberico ham hanging from the roofbeams. The servers were friendly, and the Spanish wine was flowing more smoothly with each glass. We'd finished our main course and were too full for dessert. At this point, the waiter was a bit too attentive, hovering near us and constantly checking if we needed more wine or food.

'We're fine!' I said, a bit too snappily after the third time of asking.

'Would you like the bill?' he enquired.

'Yes, pl-' Azumi said.

'No!' I interrupted.

'Are you OK?' Azumi asked. 'You're acting a bit… weird.'

'Am I? No. It must be the wine.' Then I checked myself. 'Actually, there is one thing…' I looked around. The waiter was serving some other customers and I knew that this might be my best chance. I took a breath.

'Azumi.'

'Yeah?'

Seconds passed. Or was it minutes? I breathed deeply again.

'Azumi... Will you marry me?'

About the Author

After living in four countries and working as a tour guide, journalist, baker, and occasional silver service waiter, Garett Wilson moved to Japan seven years ago. He lives in Tokyo, where he now teaches English and history at a high school.

You can contact Garett on Twitter:

@garettwilson3

If you like this book, please leave a review on Amazon. Thank you for your support.

82119620R00163

Made in the USA
Middletown, DE
31 July 2018